Aviarium

To Carolyn, Emmie and Sam – D.C.

For Mom – T.W.

BIG PICTURE PRESS

First published in the UK in 2026 by Big Picture Press,
an imprint of Bonnier Books UK
5th Floor, HYLO,
105 Bunhill Row,
London, EC1Y 8LZ

The authorised representative in the EEA
is Bonnier Books UK (Ireland) Limited.
Registered office address:
Block B, The Crescent Building
Northwood, Santry
Dublin 9, D09 C6X8, Ireland
compliance@bonnierbooks.ie
www.bonnierbooks.co.uk

1 3 5 7 9 10 8 6 4 2

ISBN 978-1-80078-779-7

This book was typeset in Gill Sans, Mrs Green and Modern20 BT.
The illustrations were created in graphite and watercolour, with colour added digitally.

Edited by Russell McLean
Designed by Winsome d'Abreu
Produced by Neil Randles

Printed in China

This book was produced in association with the RSPB.

For all RSPB licensed products sold by Bonnier Books UK Ltd,
Bonnier Books UK Ltd will donate a minimum of £1,000 to RSPB Sales Ltd,
which gives all of its distributable profits through Gift Aid to the RSPB.

RSPB

Welcome to the Museum

ENTER HERE

Aviarium

Illustrated by TEAGAN WHITE

Written by DOMINIC COUZENS

BPP

Preface

There are over 11,000 species of birds in the world and their diversity is amazing. The smallest is barely bigger than a bee, the largest nearly 3 metres tall. Most can fly in different ways, whether it be hovering, skimming waves, soaring over mountains or diving on prey at 350 kilometres per hour. Many are very intelligent, even using tools such as twigs to extract food from crevices. Some sing the most beautiful songs, others just croak. Some can even dance!

Birds play a vital role in maintaining ecosystems. Finches disperse seeds through their droppings, helping plants to spread. Insectivorous species control pests that destroy agricultural crops. Vultures clean up carrion, helping stop the spread of diseases such as rabies. Hummingbirds and honeyeaters pollinate plants. Seabirds help recycle nutrients through their droppings, fertilising coral reefs.

Sadly, many birds are in decline, with around 1,400 species threatened at a critical level. The RSPB, a charity for the conservation of birds and nature, is committed to reversing the declines of over 70 priority species in the UK and around the world. We bring people together who love and want to discover more about birds and other wildlife, and who want to take action to restore the natural world.

Dr Andy Evans
Head of Global Species Recovery,
Royal Society for the Protection of Birds

Entrance

Welcome to Aviarium

Of all the wild animals with which we share Earth, birds are the most visible. They are a part of daily life, even where we barely notice them – pigeons feed in parks, for example, and crows strut around the dusty edges of messy humanity. Their sounds stir us from sleep; their songs provide a backing track for encounters in wild spaces. From cities to deep forests, they are everywhere. We cannot avoid them. And neither should we – birds are a barometer of how we are treating the world.

Step into these galleries and allow yourself to wonder; birds are extraordinary. They have been present on Earth for just a blink of the evolutionary eye. Birds have only truly diverged from reptiles, fully feathered and lacking teeth, in the last 150 million years. But they have made the most of their time, filling every habitat apart from deep ocean and diverging into more than 11,000 living species. They have radiated into an astonishing variety of forms – from heavy, ground-based birds to long-winged masters of the ocean winds, from tree-dwelling songbirds to tiny, glittering hummingbirds. This variety is enhanced by miraculous structures, feathers, which don't just protect birds and enable them to fly, but also confer every kind of colour, from lavish to dull. Birds have evolved voices that we humans can hear easily, and every bird has its own unique vocabulary. And the range of lifestyle is also truly something amazing.

Enter *Aviarium*, the world of birds – it is wonderful.

Birds and Dinosaurs

One of the most stunning revelations of modern science has been to confirm that birds are, simply put, a group of dinosaurs. The asteroid strike of 66 million years ago wiped out all the dinosaurs with the exception of a small group of therapod dinosaurs (with three toes on each limb), which flourished and continued to evolve into the distinctive group we call birds. Modern birds are warm-blooded, feathered reptiles without teeth and with hollow bones. They are the only dinosaurs that ever flew (the pterosaurs were a different group with a very different anatomy, and not dinosaurs).

Thousands of recent fossil finds, many from China, have muddied the distinction between birds and non-avian dinosaurs. We now know, for example, that many non-flying dinosaurs bore feathers. The earliest flying birds showed typical reptilian features such as jaws with teeth, claws on the wings and a bony tail, so it has become harder, not easier, to say when the first 'bird' appeared. It is also a matter of much debate when the first bird evolved powered flight. We can be reasonably sure, though, that it happened about 150 million years ago, during the late Jurassic period.

Most people have heard of *Archaeopteryx*, perhaps the world's most famous fossil of all. Discovered in 1861 in Germany, it revealed the very first fossilised feathers. For almost a century it stood alone as a 'missing link' between dinosaurs and birds, but there are now thousands of early bird fossils from around the globe. Today, the evolution of birds is one of the most exciting and hotly debated subjects in palaeontology.

Key to plate

***1:* Protopteryx fengningensis**
Length: 20cm, including tail
Lived: 131–129 million years ago
This is a representative of a species-rich group of Cretaceous birds known as the enantiornithes, found worldwide but killed off at the same time as the non-avian dinosaurs. This species was about the size of a starling.

***2:* Confuciusornis sanctus**
Length: 28–30cm, including tail
Lived: 124–119 million years ago
Many thousands of fossils of this pigeon-sized bird have been found in China, representing males, females and young, some with longer tails than others. The abundance is likely to reflect its social structure – family groups or flocks.

***3:* Archaeopteryx lithographica**
Length: 50–56cm, including tail
Lived: 150–148 million years ago
Formerly regarded as the world's earliest bird, but now thought to be a link between avian and non-avian dinosaurs, with jaws of teeth, claws on the wing, and bones along its tail. It was about the size of a crow and lived in Central Europe.

***4:* Anchiornis huxleyi**
Length: 60–62cm, including tail
Lived: 160 million years ago
A non-avian dinosaur that managed to have more feathers than your average bird – on its body, wings and legs. There are so many specimens of this Chinese fossil that scientists have been able to work out its grey and black colouration.

***5:* Velociraptor mongoliensis**
Length: 150–200cm, including tail
Lived: 75–71 million years ago
This was a small non-avian dinosaur with feathers and a long tail, as well as an enlarged claw on each hind foot that was used to stab and pin down prey. Contrary to popular depictions, it was only turkey-sized, couldn't outrun a human and lived in the late Cretaceous, not the Jurassic period.

1
2
3
4
5

Gallery 1

Flightless Birds

Large Flightless Birds
Southern Brown Kiwi
Habitat: Grassland

Large Flightless Birds

It only takes a glance to recognise that a group of heavy-legged, tall, running flightless giants, found in the southern continents, are completely different to all other birds. Known as ratites, they form a distinct group (the Palaeognathae) that includes the world's largest and heaviest bird, the Common Ostrich. Until comparatively recent times, there were more species than there are today. The Giant Moa (*Dinornis robustus*) of New Zealand, which grew to 3.6 metres tall, was wiped out in the 15th century. *Aepyornis maximus*, a species of elephant bird from Madagascar, was both taller (at 3 metres) and much more massive than the Common Ostrich, but it has probably been extinct for 1,000 years. It laid the largest known egg of any animal, dwarfing those even of the biggest dinosaurs. The moas and the elephant birds had no wings at all.

The biggest birds in the world today, alongside the ostriches, include the rheas of South America and the emus and cassowaries of Australasia. Surprisingly, they are all thought to have evolved from ancestors that could fly, although they have lost their keel – the bone to which the pectoral muscles are attached. They all have wings of a sort, but in emus and cassowaries they are much reduced in size and invisible under the plumage.

Most of these giant birds are grazers, feeding on vegetation and wandering around open areas, often in groups. The cassowaries are the exception, being forest birds that are highly secretive and not sociable. Cassowaries eat large fruits and play a crucial role in dispersing rainforest tree seeds.

Ratites are formidable birds that are not only bulky but also well armed with heavy legs and sharp claws. They can all kick, and the cassowaries have a long, sharp inner claw that can severely injure predators and has been known to kill humans.

Curiously, in all ratites it is the male that primarily incubates and cares for the chicks. Emus may look after a brood for seven months, and cassowaries for as long as a year.

Key to plate

1a: **Emu**
1b: **Emu chick**
Dromaius novaehollandiae
Height: 150–190cm
The emu has unusual 'double' feathers, with the main shaft and a branch. It also has colourful bare skin on the head. In the breeding season it makes a booming sound.

2a: **Greater Rhea**
2b: **Greater Rhea chick**
Rhea americana
Height: 127–150cm
The rheas of the grasslands of South America have a feathered head and neck, and three toes. They have well developed wings that are used for balance when running.

3a: **Common Ostrich**
Struthio camelus
Height: 210–275cm (male), 175–190cm (female)
Ostriches are the world's largest, tallest and fastest-running birds, and the only ones with just two toes. They can reach 2.75m in height with their neck raised and run at 70km/h to escape predators such as big cats.

3b: **Common Ostrich eggs**
These eggs are the largest of any living bird, about 15cm in diameter and 17cm long. Each one weighs around 24 times more than a chicken's egg.

4: **Northern Cassowary**
Casuarius unappendiculatus
Height: 120–150cm
Cassowaries are forest dwellers with sleek, black, hairlike plumage. The function of the peculiar helmet-like casque on the top of the head is not known, but it might help the birds dig in the soil for food.

2a
1a
2b
3a
1b
3b
4

Southern Brown Kiwi

If there was a prize for the least bird-like bird, it would probably go to the kiwi, which is the world's smallest ratite. Its feathers look like hair, it obtains much of its food by smell and it cannot see particularly well. What's more, its body temperature is lower than that of other birds (37–38°C rather than 39–42°C), it is nocturnal and has no visible wings or tail.

The kiwi egg is the world's biggest by relative size, being six times larger than normal for the size of bird and amounting to 25 per cent of the female's body weight (the Common Ostrich egg is relatively the smallest). When close to laying an egg, a female kiwi has no room in her stomach for food! Once it hatches, the kiwi chick is already so well nourished that it can become independent in two weeks. Amazingly, some kiwis lay clutches of two eggs.

Uniquely among birds, the kiwi's nostrils open out at the end of its long, curved bill, rather than on the upper part of the bill near the face. Its sense of smell is very keen. It also has long bristles at the base of the bill, and a battery of highly sensitive touch receptors at the tip. This allows for excellent detection of food such as worms and insects hidden in the soil. Together with keen hearing, kiwis have a great set of senses for successful ground foraging at night.

Key to plate

1: **Southern Brown Kiwi**
Apteryx australis
Length: 50–65cm
The Southern Brown Kiwi is one of five kiwi species, all of which are found in New Zealand. They are nocturnal and make loud, wailing calls to keep in contact. Unlike most birds, kiwis mark the boundary of their territory with droppings. In the event of an incursion by another kiwi, a kicking fight breaks out, on rare occasions to the death.

2: **Nest**
Using their strong legs and claws, kiwis dig multiple burrows for their nests, often completing these many months before using them. The burrows may be a metre long and the chamber is lined with fern leaves.

3: **Eggs**
Kiwi eggs are incubated by both sexes, and sometimes other relatives chip in to assist. To break out, young kiwis have to kick through the shell of their egg. (Other birds have an egg-tooth.) The eggs have evolved antibacterial and antifungal properties to protect them in the damp underground burrows.

Habitat: Grassland

Grassland forms in the climatic zone between deserts and forests. Different grasslands around the world go by different names, such as prairies in North America and steppe in Asia. They may be dotted with lakes and pools. Grasslands with scattered trees are often called savannas.

There are broadly two types. Temperate grasslands, such as those in North America, experience 300–600 millimetres of rain annually, while tropical grasslands receive about 500–1,500 millimetres. In temperate grasslands, birds need to cope with extremes of temperature. A winter grassland can be fiercely cold, and many species migrate away.

Grasslands supply an abundance of insects and seeds – any species that can eat grass seeds is going to thrive! Some have high concentrations of herbivorous mammals, providing further feeding opportunities. Oxpeckers in Africa eat ticks from animal hides, while cattle egrets feed on insects stirred up by the feet of large animals.

Most grassland birds are camouflaged by cryptic plumage, and the majority also nest on the ground. Quite a few are expert runners or have long legs – examples include the tinamous and the bustards. By contrast, dense grassland contains few song-posts, so many of the birds here have loud songs or showy display-flights to attract a mate.

Key to plate

1: **Brown-headed Cowbird**
Molothrus ater
Length: 15–20cm
This cowbird was once confined to the Great Plains of North America, where it would follow herds of bison in order to prey on insects disturbed by their grazing. Now an abundant farmland and urban bird, it lays its eggs in the nests of other birds, with more than 200 host species known.

2: **Rosy-throated Longclaw**
Macronyx ameliae
Length: 19–20cm
A ground-living African savanna bird that has greatly elongated hind claws, which help it to walk in grass without losing balance. It eats insects gathered on the ground, and the male, like many grassland birds, often sings in flight.

3: **Secretarybird**
Sagittarius serpentarius
Length: 125–150cm
The Secretarybird stalks African savannas for insects, mammals and snakes. It kills large prey by powerful kicks of its long legs, which are densely scaled to protect from snake bites.

4: **Lesser Florican**
Sypheotides indicus
Length: 46–51cm
In the breeding season, the male Lesser Florican leaps above long grass, flaps its wings with apparent desperation, holds its legs up and drops down again – genuine wild bird comedy. The species lives in India.

5: **Spotted Nothura**
Nothura maculosa
Length: 23–26cm
This is a member of the primitive family of tinamous, closely related to ostriches. It reproduces rapidly – the female may lay four clutches of five eggs a year in the plains of central South America.

6: **Demoiselle Crane**
Anthropoides virgo
Length: 90–100cm
It breeds on the steppes of Central Asia, usually near water, and feeds mainly on seeds and insects, which it picks from the ground while walking slowly. Migrating south in winter, it travels in elegant V-formations.

7: **White Monjita**
Xolmis irupero
Length: 17–18cm
The startling white plumage stands out in the South American savanna as this bird perches boldly by tracks or on bushes. It drops down to catch insects on the ground, often hovering for long periods.

8: **Ground Tit**
Pseudopodoces humilis
Length: 19–20cm
This extraordinary bird bounds over low vegetation in long hops that make it look like a living rubber ball. It probes yak dung for insects and digs its own burrow more than a metre long for the nest. It also roosts underground.

1
2
3
4
5
6
7
8

Gallery 2

Seabirds

Albatrosses and Petrels

It's likely that every single square metre of ocean or sea on the planet has been crossed by a bird at some time, and much of that is down to the albatrosses and petrels – the great ocean travellers. Several species fly more than 50,000 kilometres in a year, and some follow migratory loops that take them from the southern oceans towards the Arctic Circle and back. They have perfected 'dynamic soaring' – using the differential between slower air just above the waves and faster air above it to whisk them upwards, and then to glide effortlessly down and make great progress with barely a wingbeat. They also use the natural updraft produced by waves to propel them above the water. These birds generally have long wings with sharp tips, the ideal shape to produce lift.

Albatrosses and petrels have unusual nostrils encased in a horny tube, as well as a large olfactory lobe in the brain. Both these features indicate a strong sense of smell. Some birds are known to make zigzagging movements upwind towards scents, and there is evidence that seabirds use smell to find their personal breeding burrows. Their scent partly comes from stomach oil, which is sometimes vomited at predators as a deterrent. The food of these birds is limited to marine animals, important types being fish, squid and plankton. Some dive down for prey from a swimming position, while others snatch food from the water's surface while flying. Many species feed at night, when prey is frequently nearer the surface.

Albatrosses and petrels are very long lived and reproduce slowly – they may even take a year off from breeding. Most lay just one egg, and both parents contribute intense effort into raising their chick.

Key to plate

1: **Short-tailed Shearwater**
Ardenna tenuirostris
Length: 40–45cm
Wingspan: 91–100cm
The Short-tailed Shearwater is one of the great travellers – after breeding, it migrates 15,000km from its Australian breeding colonies to the North Pacific, even as far as the Bering Sea. While breeding it may range up to 4,000km on a single foraging flight.

2: **Wandering Albatross**
Diomedea exulans
Length: 107–135cm
Wingspan: 254–351cm
This huge seabird has the longest wingspan of any bird, a maximum of 3.5m. Using dynamic soaring it can cover vast distances in a year, with more than 120,000km recorded.

3: **Snow Petrel**
Pagodroma nivea
Length: 30–40cm
Wingspan: 75–95cm
The Snow Petrel has completely white plumage. It is a bird of the pack-ice, feeding around icebergs and resting on them. Colonies, though, are on cliffs. It eats krill, fish and dead animals.

4a: **Laysan Albatross**
4b: **Laysan Albatross chick**
Phoebastria immutabilis
Length: 79–81cm
Wingspan: 195–203cm
The breeding season of this northern hemisphere albatross lasts 290 days. Birds pair for life and can still breed at an advanced age – 74 years and counting in the case of one female named Wisdom on Midway Atoll.

5: **Fairy Prion**
Pachyptila turtur
Length: 23–28cm
Wingspan: 56–60cm
Prions breed in colonies on small islands. To prevent predation, they visit their crevice nest only at night, to feed the chick. As a last line of defence, they are capable of spewing foul stomach oil over intruders.

6: **White-faced Storm-Petrel**
Pelagodroma marina
Length: 18–21cm
Wingspan: 38–45cm
No bigger than starlings, storm-petrels cope with everything the ocean throws at them. They spend most of their time flitting over the water, dipping down to snatch krill and other planktonic crustaceans, as well as small fish.

1
2
3
4a
4b
5
6

Tropical Seabirds

Most seabird species are found in high latitudes, where the wind helps them to fly and the fierce ocean currents stir up nutrients from the bottom of the sea. The tropics are calmer and more benign. Albatrosses, for example, which need strong winds to take off and fly, cannot live here at all. There are still some productive cold currents in tropical regions, such as the Humboldt Current off western South America, which reaches the Galapagos, but generally there is less food and fewer birds.

There are some exciting tropical seabirds, though, perhaps none more so than frigatebirds. Amazingly, their plumage isn't waterproof, so they simply fly over the ocean for days on end and snatch what they need from the water surface, or dexterously swoop on flying fish in the air. They are great pirates too, snatching hard-earned meals from other seabirds returning to their colonies. Recent studies have shown that frigatebirds, which are the world's lightest birds for their size, use thermals under cumulus clouds to maintain their position high above the water (2,500–4,000m). They take naps on the wing, with one hemisphere of the brain remaining awake. Just for a few minutes each day they fly down to feed from the sea.

Terns are also great travellers that prefer not to get wet. It is thought that juvenile Sooty Terns (*Onychoprion fuscatus*) stay airborne for their first four years at least, possibly never landing, although they do stand on ocean flotsam. Noddies have a similar lifestyle.

Tropicbirds and boobies are wanderers too, but do routinely swim on the ocean surface. Both will fly very high above the water, but are full-immersion plunge-divers when hunting. However, once again, they will sometimes catch flying fish in mid-air.

All of these tropical seabirds usually nest in colonies, especially on remote, undisturbed islands.

Key to plate

1: **Brown Pelican**
Pelecanus occidentalis
Length: 100–137cm
Wingspan: about 200cm
Unusual for being a marine pelican, this species often plunge-dives into the ocean head-first in order to scoop up fish prey into its enormous pouch. The bill acts as a net and can hold up to 10 litres of water.

2: **Brown Booby**
Sula leucogaster
Length: 68–80cm
Wingspan: 132–155cm
The boobies are famous for their spectacular plunge-dives into the sea from a height of up to 15m. They also dive in at shallower angles, all for obtaining the fish (ranging in size from 3 to 40cm) that make up their diet.

3: **White-tailed Tropicbird**
Phaethon lepturus
Length: 60–80cm, including tail of 30–40cm
Wingspan: 90–95cm
This elegant bird spends hours flying over the ocean, often far from land. It plunge-dives for flying fish and squid. Tropicbirds have serrated bills, allowing them to hold on to these slippery catches.

4: **Brown Noddy**
Anous stolidus
Length: 38–40cm
Wingspan: 77–85cm
The noddy is named for its courtship display, in which male and female nod their pale caps at each other. This species nests widely on islands and ranges all over the tropical ocean, feeding on fish and squid.

5: **Great Frigatebird**
Fregata minor
Length: 85–105cm
Wingspan: 205–230cm
Frigatebirds spend much time aloft, either catching flying fish that break the surface or chasing other seabirds to bully them into giving up food. Males inflate their colourful neck pouch during the courtship display.

6a: **White Tern**
6b: **White Tern chick**
Gygis alba
Length: 23–33cm
Wingspan: 70–87cm
The White Tern is famous for making no nest at all. On tropical islets, it simply lays a single egg in a depression or fork on a tree branch or, sometimes, on small coral rocks. The chick has evolved strong claws to hold on.

1
2
3
4
5
6a
6b

Habitat: Cliffs and Islands

Seabirds are highly adapted to the marine environment, but because they have to lay eggs and incubate them, they must at some point go to dry land to breed. This presents problems, because land doesn't suit them. They have webbed feet, which makes perching awkward, and their legs are often set far back on the body. This supplies propulsion in water, but may make walking difficult. Many have long wings, making the mechanics of approaching land tricky.

Seabirds' discomfort on land means that they are exceptionally vulnerable to ground predators, usually mammals such as rats. This often limits them to breeding in places that either lack predators, such as islands, or sites that are hazardous to predators, such as tall cliffs and precipices. The limited availability of such sites means that the visitors all have to pack together, and virtually all seabirds are colonial.

Not every cliff or island will do. The location must be close to the sea, and it must be within reasonable reach of rich fishing areas. Many seabirds will commute up to about 50 kilometres, sometimes much further, but if food is too far away, feeding young may be impossible.

With so much crowding, it isn't surprising that different birds occupy different parts of islands or cliffs. Some live on boulders close to the sea, while others pack on to narrow ledges on tall cliffs. Crevices, holes or burrows are sought-after refuges for many species, while others, especially bigger birds, require flat, wide ledges – these may need to be windy to help them take off. Sea caves may be ideal, as may grassland above cliffs, or very low, sandy islands. One of the great delights of this habitat is seeing many types of seabirds, each contributing to the noise, smell and general melee.

Key to plate

1: **Red-legged Kittiwake**
Rissa brevirostris
Length: 37cm
Three-quarters of the world population of this small gull (200,000 pairs) breeds on St George Island in the Aleutians, on towering cliffs. It hunts over deep Arctic waters, catching fish near the surface.

2: **Guanay Cormorant**
Leucocarbo bougainvilliorum
Length: 71–76cm
Cormorants are seabirds but their plumage is only semi-waterproof. The feathers become soaked, reducing their buoyancy and making diving more efficient. After swimming, they must hold their wings out to dry. This bird is named after the guano that builds up at its colonies, once a major source of fertiliser.

3: **Crested Auklet**
Aethia cristatella
Length: 23–27cm
A seabird of the North Pacific that breeds in large colonies on cliffs. Remarkably, it produces a tangerine-like body odour in the breeding season that helps in attracting a mate. The scent can be detected by humans far away from the breeding islands.

4: **Atlantic Puffin**
Fratercula arctica
Length: 26–29cm
The remarkable bill of the Atlantic Puffin, with its backward-facing spines, allows the bird to grip multiple fish at a time to deliver to the young. These are held against the roof of the mouth by the spiny tongue.

5: **Southern Rockhopper Penguin**
Eudyptes chrysocome
Length: 51–62cm
Being flightless, penguins can only breed on cliffs or rocks accessible from the ocean. These birds progress up slopes with two-footed hops. The Southern Rockhopper lays two eggs, although usually only one hatches.

1
2
3
4
5

Gallery 3

Waterbirds

Ducks, Geese and Swans
Long-legged Wading Birds
Kingfishers
Shorebirds
Habitat: Rivers

Ducks, Geese and Swans

Water might flow off a duck's back, but it is also key to every member of this family. Often known as waterfowl, these birds live by fresh water and thrive in all its many habitats, but some species spend all or part of their lives by the sea. All waterfowl have webbed feet and swim well, with many species habitually diving underwater, propelled by their feet and only rarely using their wings. Many have dense plumage that is made waterproof by their preen-oil.

As a rule, ducks, geese and swans have quite heavy, flattened bodies, with a long neck, large head and a heavy bill. The bill is broad and flat and has a nail at the tip, which helps the birds to grip food and also to fine-tune exploration in the mud or water, aided by sensitive touch receptors. The bill has comb-like lamellae on the sides of both the upper and lower mandibles, allowing the birds to strain small particles of food out of the water as it exits the bill. Waterfowl eat all kinds of food, from fish to grass.

Most waterfowl are powerful fliers – some species are among the fastest in level flight – and they are capable of migrating long distances. By complete contrast, one or two species are flightless, and many waterfowl moult all their flight feathers simultaneously after breeding, preventing them from flying for a few weeks. Some move to special safe places just to moult. When flying, waterfowl often assume impressive V-formations in flocks. This pattern saves energy for the birds behind the bird ahead.

Many waterfowl pluck their own breast feathers to line their nests with down, and as a rule, they lay large clutches of eggs. Very soon after the youngsters hatch, they are mobile and follow their parent to water.

Key to plate

1a: **Mallard male**
1b: **Mallard female**
1c: **Mallard ducklings**
Anas platyrhynchos
Length: 50–65cm
The origin of most domestic ducks around the world, the Mallard is also one of the most abundant, at least in the northern hemisphere. It is hardy, highly adaptable and at ease in human environments.

2: **Bar-headed Goose**
Anser indicus
Length: 71–76cm
These geese are famous for flying over the Himalayas on migration from Central Asia to India, reaching 6,000m regularly (and 10,000m claimed). To do so, they have a special type of haemoglobin in the blood that absorbs oxygen efficiently at this height.

3: **Trumpeter Swan**
Cygnus buccinator
Length: 139–157cm
Weight: 10–13kg
Swans are among the largest and heaviest flying birds and require a considerable run-up to get airborne. They may have 25,000 feathers on the body. The long neck enables them to reach down to the bottom of fairly deep water.

4a: **African Pygmy-Goose male**
4b: **African Pygmy-Goose female**
Nettapus auritus
Length: 27–33cm
The smallest of waterfowl, African Pygmy-Geese nest in holes in trees and spend most of their time in water, feeding on seeds and other vegetation, especially water lilies. They also eat insects and small fish.

5: **Pink-eared Duck**
Malacorhynchus membranaceus
Length: 36–45cm
The Australian Pink-eared Duck has a specialised bill for filtering small organisms. The bill is swollen at the front to let water in, while the sides have fleshy lamellae that sieve out edible items.

6: **Common Eider**
Somateria mollissima
Length: 50–71cm
This duck is famous for lining its nest with exceptionally dense, insulating feathers – so-called 'eider down'. The bird itself lives in shallow seas and dives for shellfish, which it crushes with its heavy bill.

1a
1b
1c
2
3
4a
4b
5
6

Long-legged Wading Birds

The world's shallows are ripe for long-legged hunters that are prepared to wade, and over millions of years quite a number of families have evolved to cash in on this opportunity. All of them are large birds, and all have long legs to get them into open water or the vegetation at its fringes. They are set apart by the shape of the bill, their method of hunting and their diet.

The range of potential food in shallow water, both fresh and salty, is enormous. It includes fish, amphibians, small birds and mammals, molluscs, crustaceans and more. Some wading birds take a range of these, while others are more specialised. Flamingos feed on plant seeds and algae, along with crustaceans, while the Limpkin (*Aramus guarauna*) feeds almost exclusively on snails.

Among the group, there are those that feed by sight and those that rely principally on touch. There is some crossover. Herons and egrets are well known for their ability to stand still in or next to water for a long time, until a fish or frog comes into view at their feet. At this point, with their specially adapted S-shaped neck, they make a lightning-fast grab. The Roseate Spoonbill is equally patient but then lunges its whole body forwards to entrap large fish. Storks tend to simply wander around and pick up visible items straightforwardly in their very large, straight bills. Ibises and spoonbills are touch feeders. Ibises have long, curved bills with very sensitive tips, while spoonbills have flattened ends to their bills. They swish them from side to side in murky water in an attempt to feel and rapidly snatch fish and other animals.

Most long-legged wading birds nest in colonies and many build impressive nests, often out of sticks in trees. Flamingos build remarkable mud-mounds to keep their eggs above the salt water.

Key to plate

1: **Greater Flamingo**
Phoenicopterus roseus
Length: 120–125cm
Flamingos are famous for their long legs and necks, and pink plumage derived from pigments in their diet, mainly from crustaceans. The bill, with its characteristic bend to keep it evenly open, allows the birds to filter small items suspended in water. The birds always feed upside down.

2: **Great Egret**
Ardea alba
Length: 80–104cm
This widepsread egret is a forager of fish, amphibians, crustaceans and small mammals in both salt and fresh water. It occurs across the Americas, Asia, Africa and southern Europe.

3: **Shoebill**
Balaeniceps rex
Length: 120cm
The remarkable 'clog-like' bill of this huge heron-like bird has evolved to grab very large fish, especially lungfish, that languish in the muddy shallows of Central African papyrus swamps.

4: **Roseate Spoonbill**
Platalea ajaja
Length: 71–86cm
Improbably pink, the Roseate Spoonbill is found mainly in South America. To feed, it wades in the water, moving its partially opened bill from side to side in an attempt to detect fish by touch, at which point the bill slams shut.

5: **Scarlet Ibis**
Eudocimus ruber
Length: 56–71cm
An exquisitely coloured wading bird that probes the water with its long, curved bill, mainly for crustaceans. It occurs in both freshwater and marine habitats, including mangroves, and often nests in spectacular large colonies in trees.

6: **White Stork**
Ciconia ciconia
Length: 100–102cm
The White Stork's massive bill enables it to pick off frogs, crayfish, small mammals and other prey as it wanders in grass and marshes. The birds build a huge stick nest, 2–3m wide and deep, often on a building.

1
2
3
4
5
6

Kingfishers

The best-known members of this family are celebrated for their dramatic plunge-dives into water to snatch fish, but kingfishers as a whole have a wide range of habitats and feeding strategies. The Laughing Kookaburra of Australia, for example, catches a range of small animals in the bush, often far from water, and many other species of kingfisher live in forests.

All kingfishers, though, are perch-hunters, watching for prey from an elevated position. The eyes don't move much within their sockets, so kingfishers often bob their heads and move them from side to side to keep focused. Those that hunt over water must compensate for refraction – the bending of light when it passes from water to air – when they dive. Kingfishers have a large head and a disproportionately long, straight bill which enables them to grab what they spot. They often stun fish and other animals by beating them against a perch repeatedly. For a bird that spends hours perching, their feet are surprisingly short and weak.

The kingfisher family is highly successful and is found all over the world. Many species are extremely colourful, with bold patterns and glistening iridescence.

All members of the family use holes for nesting, which they usually dig out themselves, and for this purpose kingfishers' second and third toes are partially fused together. Even in small species, nesting tunnels often measure a metre or so long. Most species excavate earth banks, but tree holes and even termite mounds can be taken over as a suitable nesting site.

Key to plate

1: **Stork-billed Kingfisher**
Pelargopsis capensis
Length: 35–41cm
With its powerful bill, this species has a broad diet encompassing fish, insects, small mammals and crabs, as well as frogs. Larger prey is beaten to death on the perch before consumption.

2: **Laughing Kookaburra**
Dacelo novaeguineae
Length: 39–42cm
An unusual member of the family that often lives far from water, even in Australian cities and backyards. Its famous 'laughing' call is uttered especially at dawn, often a duet between male and female.

3: **Common Paradise-Kingfisher**
Tanysiptera galatea
Length: 33–43cm, including streamers
The unusual nesting site of this New Guinea kingfisher is a termite colony in the trees, where the birds will dig a tunnel up to 15cm long, despite attempts by the insects to repair it.

4: **Common Kingfisher**
Alcedo atthis
Length: 16–17cm
Found widely in Eurasia, this is a small species that flies rapidly on whirring wings low down over the water surface. It specialises in hunting fish, which it catches with a plunge-dive before swallowing head-first.

5: **Pied Kingfisher**
Ceryle rudis
Length: 25–30cm
Common in Africa and Asia, this kingfisher typically hunts by hovering over the water before diving in. Most unusually, it is sociable, with breeding pairs living in clusters.

6: **Ringed Kingfisher**
Megaceryle torquata
Length: 38–42cm
This is a big kingfisher of South and Central America. It will often sit on an elevated perch above fresh water for anything between ten minutes and two hours, eventually diving down head-first with a splash.

1
2
3
4
5
6

Shorebirds

As their name implies, this group of birds are usually encountered on beaches, seashores and estuaries. They are often scurrying around at the water's edge, picking up items from the mud. There is scarcely a shoreline in the world, or indeed the border of a lake or marsh, where these birds don't occur.

Shorebirds are small to medium sized, usually with long legs. They walk or run, but don't usually hop. They have eyes set on the side of the head, allowing some species virtually 360° panoramic vision. Most have long and narrow wings, which helps them fly fast and far. Many species undertake epic migrations of thousands of kilometres, often flying at great altitudes (3,000 metres).

Shorebirds are famous for the variety in their bills. Curlews have long, downcurved bills ideal for probing, while stints have short, straight bills for picking from the surface. The plovers have large eyes and short, heavy bills, making them suited to watching the surface for moving food. Many shorebirds probe into the mud or sand and have batteries of touch receptors at the bill tip.

All shorebirds are drawn to open areas. Many breed at high latitudes, especially in the Arctic, but some are confined to mountains. Their breeding systems are astonishing in their variety. In some species, such as oystercatchers, both parents expend efforts rearing the young; in some sandpipers, a female may lay up to four clutches, each incubated by a different male. In Ruffs, the males play no part in breeding other than mating.

Shorebirds are famous for the displays they perform to lure predators away from the nest. Many pretend to have a broken wing or will incubate a 'nest' that doesn't exist. Others pretend to be rodents, crouching down and squeaking to distract the danger.

Key to plate

1: **Bar-tailed Godwit**
Limosa lapponica
Length: 37–39cm
North American Bar-tailed Godwits undertake the longest nonstop migration of any landbird. Individuals leave Alaska and may fly to Australia or New Zealand. One bird is known to have travelled 13,560km (Alaska to Tasmania) without pausing or landing.

2: **Red Phalarope**
Phalaropus fulicarius
Length: 20–22cm
A very unusual shorebird that lives out in the ocean in winter, swimming like a duck and feeding on plankton. It often spins around to create a vortex that drags prey upwards and within range. When breeding, the duller-coloured male is responsible for incubation and tending the young.

3: **American Avocet**
Recurvirostra americana
Length: 43–47cm
A tall shorebird that wades in water, the American Avocet swings its unusual bill from side to side in order to detect items in suspension, usually shrimps and flies, which it then swallows. It can also swim well.

4: **Common Ringed Plover**
Charadrius hiaticula
Length: 18–20cm
Plovers are sight-feeders, scanning the surface while standing still, then running to grab any edible matter spotted. Common Ringed Plovers have so-called 'disruptive camouflage', with bold plumage patterns that disguise the outline of their body.

5: **Ruff**
Calidris pugnax
Length: 20–32cm
In the spring, male Ruffs moult into extraordinarily variable plumage, with over 800 patterns described. Males then display silently together at a lek, and females visit to choose a male with whom to mate. Females are responsible for all nesting behaviour.

6: **Far Eastern Curlew**
Numenius madagascariensis
Length: 53–66cm
Curlews are famous for their long, downcurved bills, which are longer in females than males. These are perfect for probing into soft sand and, with a wide turning circle at the tip, for getting into hard-to-reach crevices and fissures.

7: **Ruddy Turnstone**
Arenaria interpres
Length: 21–26cm
Turnstones are superbly camouflaged against seaweed-cloaked rocks and pebbly beaches, where they earn their name by flicking stones and other objects over to reveal edible items hidden beneath. Several birds may cooperate in dislodging larger items.

1
2
3
4
5
6
7

Habitat: Rivers

Rivers don't form one single habitat, but many. In their 'younger stages', near the source, they may be tumbling, rushing streams in hilly areas. As they head for the coast, they mature to become sluggish meanders, before spilling into the sea as estuaries. The middle of the river provides a different habitat to the banks, and the catchment of a river may form a floodplain. Rivers also form waterfalls, and oxbow lakes when a meander is cut off. Slow, sluggish rivers may differ little from ponds or lakes in what they offer. All in all, rivers provide a wide range of opportunities for many birds.

The most specialised river birds have adapted to turbulent water. It is a physically demanding environment, not very rich, but with few competitors. It is inhabited by a few ducks, the most famous of which is the Torrent Duck (*Merganetta armata*) of South America. It has a slim body, stiff tail and large webbed feet, with strong muscles to fight the current, keeping it in place to find food underwater. The widespread dippers are the only songbirds adapted to a submerged diet. They have strong claws to keep their grip on rocks and other surfaces underwater, plus very dense plumage and a large preen gland for waterproofing. Like the Torrent Duck, they feed on aquatic insects and their larvae. Several other species feed on insects beside fast-flowing streams, including the forktails of Asia.

Beyond this stage, the banks of rivers often host swallows and kingfishers, while parrots may come to nourish themselves at clay licks in the tropics. Many birds flourish at the edges of large rivers, and the biggest rivers – the Amazon, for example – may create a specific habitat of seasonally flooded forests. All birds breeding by rivers need to adapt to the possibility of the rise and fall of water levels.

Key to plate

1: **Sunbittern**
Eurypyga helias
Length: 43–48cm
An unusual bird that feeds secretively on frogs and crustaceans along the mud edges of tropical American rivers. When alarmed or displaying, the Sunbittern suddenly reveals its extraordinary open-wing pattern, which looks like two giant eyes.

2: **Waterfall Swift**
Hydrochous gigas
Length: 16cm
This rare species always nests by waterfalls in pristine rainforest, usually in small colonies. The nest is made from mosses and liverworts plucked in flight, held together by saliva and placed on walls or ledges in the spray.

3: **Hoatzin**
Opisthocomus hoazin
Length: 60–66cm
This oddity nests in bushes overhanging rivers and lakes. If the young fall out, they can swim and, uniquely, two claws on each wing enable them to climb back up. Hoatzins eat leaves and almost nothing else.

4: **Australian Pelican**
Pelecanus conspicillatus
Length: 152–188cm
Bill length: 34.6–50cm
A bird of the broad reaches of rivers, often at river mouths, where it uses its bill as a scoop net. It often feeds cooperatively, with many birds scooping at the same time, corralling and panicking the fish.

5: **American Dipper**
Cinclus mexicanus
Length: 14–20cm
True outliers among songbirds, dippers are aquatic, living alongside and within rushing water. They can immerse themselves fully to feed on insect larvae on the bottom. They sometimes nest behind waterfalls.

6a: **Moorhen**
6b: **Moorhen chicks**
Gallinula chloropus
Length: 30–38cm
Living in the dense vegetation bordering rivers and lakes, the Moorhen has long legs with remarkably long toes, which can grip on to plants and also spread out the bird's weight. It swims well, too.

1
2
3
4
5
6a
6b

Gallery 4

Birds of Prey

Day-flying Birds of Prey
Andean Condor
Owls
Habitat: Mountains

Day-flying Birds of Prey

With hooked bills, superb vision and sharp claws on powerful talons, birds of prey – also known as raptors – are supremely efficient predators. While many other birds eat living things, raptors have caught people's imagination in the dramatic and spectacular ways they do it. Hawks ambush smaller birds, Peregrine Falcons dive from the sky at astonishing speeds, Golden Eagles may chase smaller animals over cliffs, Ospreys plunge-dive and Short-toed Eagles hover over hillsides looking for snakes.

Many raptors catch birds and small mammals, but others specialise in lizards, crabs, grubs or dragonflies. Some bird-catchers prefer to prey on nestlings, others catch migrating birds in the evening. Some ambush small mammals at the entrance to their burrows and others pluck sloths out of trees; some snatch bats at cave entrances. Others don't even kill, but eat dead animals, a lifestyle known as scavenging. Raptors range in size from starling-sized (falconets) to swan-sized (eagles and vultures).

These birds have some impressive adaptations. Their eye for detail at distance (acuity) is at least twice as good as a human's. Their bills are sometimes fitted with a 'tooth' to cut the spinal cord of prey. Their claws are so sharp that it is the talons, rather than the bill, that delivers the fatal injury. And their range of wing and tail shapes allows for all kinds of flight – hovering, diving, quartering (flying low and slow) and soaring.

Day-flying birds of prey occur over the whole world and in every land habitat. They are often easiest to see in the middle of the day, when they habitually soar and may rise on thermal drafts. A quirk is that females are almost always larger than males, perhaps because they spend more time defending the nest while the male is out foraging.

Key to plate

1: **Harpy Eagle**
Harpia harpyja
Length: 87–107cm
Wingspan: 183–224cm
The world's largest eagle, with a huge, hooked bill and talons the width of a human wrist. It occurs sparingly in tropical American rainforest, where it feeds on sloths and primates.

2: **Osprey**
Pandion haliaetus
Length: 55–58cm
Wingspan: 150–180cm
The ultimate fish-catcher, obtaining food in a spectacular plunge-dive that may start 40m above water. Prey may be as much as 35cm long, carried in the talons lengthwise like a torpedo.

3: **Crested Serpent-Eagle**
Spilornis cheela
Length: 50–74cm
This raptor specialises in hunting snakes, both on the ground and in trees. Found in warmer parts of Asia, it spends hours waiting on a perch, before dropping rapidly down on prey.

4: **Pearl Kite**
Gampsonyx swainsonii
Length: 20–28cm
As small as a dove, this tropical American micro-raptor has an unusual element in its diet – lizards. To catch them, it sits on an elevated perch, watching below, then dives down to snatch the reptile in its talons.

5: **Peregrine Falcon**
Falco peregrinus
Length: 36–48cm
A record breaker in every sense, not least as the world's fastest-moving animal, reaching up to 360km/h in a vertical dive. It also occurs in every continent except Antarctica, and probably hunts more species of birds, its main diet, than any other animal.

6: **European Honey Buzzard**
Pernis apivorus
Length: 53–60cm
Wingspan: up to 150cm
Unusually, this raptor subsists largely on the larvae of wasps and bees, with some adult insects too. Dense plumage on its head guards against stings.

7: **Sharp-shinned Hawk**
Accipiter striatus
Length: 24–34cm
Ninety per cent of this hawk's diet consists of small birds, which it captures by stealth with a sudden dash at the kill. It has long toes fitted with sharp claws, which both hold and despatch prey. Females are larger and eat bigger prey.

1
2
3
4
5
6
7

Andean Condor

The Andean Condor is massive, one of the largest flying birds in the world, with a wingspan that may exceed 3 metres. It also has a formidable bill with fearsome cutting edges that enable it to slice through the thick hides of large animals, and its head and neck are bare so that it doesn't have to soak its feathers with blood and body fluids. Yet the Andean Condor is not a killer but a scavenger. It won't attack you, but it will wait patiently until you are dead!

Few birds fly with the effortless grace of this mighty condor. Its entire lifestyle depends on spotting carcasses, often from high in the sky. Each day it waits until thermals have formed in its territory, or it can work mountain updrafts, and it may then stay aloft riding the rising winds for the whole day, travelling 200 kilometres or more with scarcely a wingbeat. In the Andes, its core range, it eats llamas, alpacas, deer and rheas. On the coast, it feasts on dead seals and cetaceans. In many parts of its range, it also takes advantage of domestic animals that have come to grief.

Carcasses are a scarce resource, so once they have found them, Andean Condors must take advantage. They are adapted to gobbling down large amounts of food at once and may become flightless after a large meal. They have relatively short, non-predatory claws and are unable to carry food away with them. Even when confined to the ground, they have few enemies. They are even capable of robbing a puma of its kill, especially when more than one bird meets at a carcass.

Most Andean Condors breed at great altitude, between 3,000 and 5,000 metres. They lay one or two eggs on a flat surface, usually well up on a cliff. They also roost at great altitude, where the ultraviolet rays of the sun disinfect their soiled facial skin.

Key to plate

***1:* Andean Condor male**
Vultur gryphus
Length: 100–130cm
Wingspan: 260–320cm
Equipped with superb eyesight, condors search over vast areas to find food, looking out for carcasses or other raptors gathered on the ground or circling in the sky. Powerful gut bacteria make them immune to putrid flesh.

***2:* Andean Condor chick**
There is just one chick, which remains in the nest for six months. A young Andean Condor's plumage changes from brown to black-and-white at the age of six to eight years.

***3:* Wings**
The long, broad wings are perfectly adapted for soaring, allowing an Andean Condor to flap its wings as little as once per hour. Long 'slots' near the wingtips help reduce drag as the bird glides.

***4:* Andean Condor female**
Females are smaller and lack the male's head comb, wattle and colourful red head.

Owls

Owls are among the most recognisable of all birds. They also make some of the world's most evocative natural sounds, their far-carrying hoots an unmistakable part of the night-time atmosphere.

They fill the nocturnal niche of raptorial, hunting birds. They prey on a wide range of birds, mammals, reptiles and insects, even some fish and frogs. In common with day-flying birds of prey, they have a sharp, pointed bill and formidable talons. They tend to drop down on to prey from a height, talons first, and the sharp claws do the killing.

Owls have many adaptations to their lifestyle. They have very large, forward-facing eyes, which gives them overlapping ('binocular') vision and excellent judgement of distance, and their retinas are packed with rod cells, which confer excellent contrast in low light. The average owl can see roughly twice as well as a human in the dark. They are far from blind in daylight, however, and will often exploit artificial light sources such as streetlamps. Many hunt at dusk and dawn. Some are active by day.

Some species, though, can hunt successfully in complete darkness, and they owe this astounding ability to their hearing. Quite commonly, one ear (often the left) is placed slightly lower on the skull than the other. Directional hearing relies on the fractional difference between one ear receiving a sound signal and the other receiving the same. By having non-symmetrical ears, owls can detect differentials in both the horizontal and vertical planes. As a result they can pinpoint sounds, such as a mouse's squeak, with great accuracy. Meanwhile, the facial discs of owls help to deflect incoming sound waves towards the ears. Incidentally, the long 'ears' of many owls are simply tufts of feathers.

The other well-known adaptation of owls is their soft feathering, which makes them look 'cuddly'. Owl feathers are generally large and the flight feathers are covered with velvet-like structures that dampen noise. Serrations along the edge of the main flight feathers stabilise the flow of air. All these adaptations allow owls to fly almost silently, so that they can hear prey but prey cannot hear them.

Key to plate

1: **Pel's Fishing-Owl**
Scotopelia peli
Length: 51–61cm
This really is an owl that fishes, at night. It perches a few metres above a river or pool and flies down to snatch fish from just below the water surface. It lives in Africa.

2: **Barn Owl**
Tyto alba
Length: 33–39cm
These owls can hunt in total darkness using hearing alone. They spend much time flying low over open ground and dense vegetation, plunging down talons-first when they detect motion.

3: **Spot-bellied Eagle-Owl**
Ketupa nipalensis
Length: 51–63cm
This is a big, powerful species that eats large birds and mammals such as hares, civets and giant squirrels. The fantastic ear-tufts have nothing to do with hearing, but can be raised when the bird is excited. They may also break up the head-shape in low light, helping the owl to evade predators.

4: **Great Grey Owl**
Strix nebulosa
Length: 61–84cm
This impressive owl boasts the ability to catch voles under snow, using its extraordinary hearing to locate them, and the power of its talons to 'punch' up to 60cm through the surface.

5: **Burrowing Owl**
Athene cunicularia
Length: 19–25cm
This owl species breaks the mould by being active during the day as well as at night, and also by frequently nesting in loose colonies. It lives in burrows vacated by small mammals such as ground squirrels.

1
2
3
4
5

Habitat: Mountains

There are uplands and mountains all around the world, and everywhere they have a profound effect on the birdlife. Compared to lowlands, uplands are home to a different suite of birds, and how different those birds are depends on altitude. In the equatorial tropics, a change in height of only a few hundred metres may equate to a habitat distinct enough to have its own specialised birds and plants. Many northern Andean species, for example, are confined to a narrow altitudinal range. Throughout the world, a succession of habitats are encountered as you rise – from lush forests to dwarf forest, scrub and finally open meadows and mountain tundra.

As land rises, the climate changes in various ways. The air is thinner and it is inevitably cooler. In seasonal climates, the cold of winter can trigger some birds to retreat further downhill, a behaviour known as altitudinal migration. Those that remain often have denser plumage. The higher up, the greater the challenges. Truly alpine areas are windy, the sun is more intense and there is more ultraviolet radiation. Birds always need shelter, and especially for the nest. Many mountain birds nest in snug crevices, holes, burrows in the ground or in caves. Nest structures are often more substantial than those made by similar species at lower altitude.

The thinner air puts pressure on the body. Upland birds tend to have larger hearts and lungs, and many have higher concentrations of red blood cells to cope with lower levels of oxygen. Some have broader wings, and they may also lay down greater body fat deposits. The turbulent winds at high altitude, together with an abundance of inaccessible nest sites, may result in strong populations of raptors, which spend much of their time aloft. General inaccessibility also tends to reduce human disturbance.

Despite the challenges, lots of birds are found on mountains and many of them are colourful and spectacular.

Key to plate

1: **Yellow-billed Chough**
Pyrrhocorax graculus
Length: 34–38cm
This member of the crow family has been recorded at an altitude of 8,235m, and it regularly breeds at 5,000m or above. It lives in flocks and flies with great energy and grace.

2: **Grandala**
Grandala coelicolor
Length: 19–23cm
The scientific name means 'sky-blue', which barely justifies the astonishing colour of this Himalayan beauty. It breeds at altitudes up to 5,500m on boulder-strewn slopes and is often seen in flocks.

3: **Wallcreeper**
Tichodroma muraria
Length: 15.5–17cm
Found in high mountains in Eurasia, the Wallcreeper flicks its butterfly-like wings as it climbs up rock faces, searching for insects and spiders in cracks and fissures, often near water.

4: **Apapane**
Himatione sanguinea
Length: 13cm
Living in high-altitude forest in its native Hawaii has saved the Apapane from probable extinction. Above 1,250m there are no mosquitoes to spread avian malaria, a killer of many related species.

5a: **Alpine Accentor**
5b: **Alpine Accentor chicks**
Prunella collaris
Length: 15–19cm
This high-altitude species has a complicated breeding strategy: males and females may each have multiple partners in shared territories.

6: **White-browed Tit-Warbler**
Leptopoecile sophiae
Length: 8.5–10cm
A small, jewel-like bird of montane scrub and forest in the Himalayas. Even in winter it doesn't venture below about 2,000m.

1
2
3
4
5b
5a
6

Gallery 5

Ground Birds

Pheasants and Grouse
Superb Lyrebird
Habitat: Desert

Pheasants and Grouse

The world's greatest variety of ground-living birds is found among the pheasants and grouse, along with their relatives the partridges, turkeys, junglefowl and quails. They are all plump-bodied, with short, strong legs and feet, often with sharp claws. Some males are equipped with spurs on their legs for fighting. They have short, broad, rounded wings. They can all fly, and do so in a distinctive way – a rocketing take-off with rapid, noisy flaps and a vocal commotion. They rarely go far, however, because the energy required to lift their bodies is rapidly dissipated and they soon flop back into cover on the ground. There are exceptions – some tiny quails may migrate hundreds of kilometres – but they are all more comfortable running and walking. Some, such as the Sooty Grouse (*Dendragapus fuliginosus*) migrate some of their way on foot.

Many members of this group possess extravagant plumage, especially among the males, and birds such as peafowl, the tragopans and many pheasants are among the most opulently plumaged birds in the world. Many enhance their impression by performing complex courtship displays. Male grouse often perform communally on traditional display grounds, a system known as a lek. They self-select by skirmishing and making unusual calls such as rattles, coos or pops. The best males then mate with all the visitors.

Grouse often feed in trees, but the rest of the group scratch and dig for food on the ground, using the feet and bill. The bill is short and powerful, with a hook at the tip. Most feed primarily on plant material, but the larger species often eat invertebrates, especially in the breeding season, and occasionally even snakes and lizards.

They place their nests on the ground and are famous for sitting very still on the nest, not moving and relying on camouflage to protect them; often the less colourful female is responsible for incubation. They tend to lay a lot of eggs – the clutches of partridges, up to 15 eggs, are among the largest of any birds in the world.

Key to plate

1a: **Wild Turkey female**
1b: **Wild Turkey male**
Meleagris gallopavo
Length: 91–120cm
The Wild Turkey is native to North America. Despite its size, it is very elusive, shy and able to run away at speed. It roosts at night in trees.

2: **Indian Peafowl**
Pavo cristatus
Length: 95–115cm, but male up to 225cm with train
Famous for its loud, exclamatory call and the male's extraordinary feather train, this peafowl is a common bird on the Indian subcontinent. It is omnivorous and often eats snakes and lizards.

3: **Mountain Quail**
Oreortyx pictus
Length: 27–31cm
A species that is famously elusive, as are many species of pheasants and grouse. In the mountains of western North America, it hides away on the ground in dense shrubbery.

4: **Greater Sage-Grouse**
Centrocercus urophasianus
Length: 50–75cm
In spring, adult male sage-grouse display in leks at dawn, each bird inflating its oesophageal pouch and spreading its tail in a fan, then making curious cooing and plopping sounds. The females visit the lek and almost always mate with the superior male.

5: **Temminck's Tragopan**
Tragopan temminckii
Length: 58–64cm
Many pheasants rival peacocks for their amazing displays. Temminck's Tragopan inflates the horns on its head, as well as its blue throat lappet, beats its wings on the ground and then stands up as tall as it can.

6: **Helmeted Guineafowl**
Numida meleagris
Length: 53–63cm
Native to Africa, these birds are seen in flocks. Like several species in this group of ground-living birds, they are also domesticated worldwide. Members of flocks may circle round young birds to protect them from predators.

1a
3
2
1b
5
4
6

Superb Lyrebird

Many birds are heard before they are seen, but in the case of the Superb Lyrebird, you tend to hear the 'wrong' bird before you see it. That's because this unique songbird of eastern Australia is one of the world's most accurate bird mimics. About three-quarters of its loud song consists of imitations, and in any given location it will copy 25 per cent of all species present in the moist temperate and subtropical forest where it lives. It has an extraordinary ability to broadcast the sound of a whole flock of birds, including a chorus of kookaburras. It can do a rendition of trees creaking in the wind, and occasionally human sounds, too.

The song is part of the Superb Lyrebird's impressive display. The rest is like that of a peacock that ran out of money for bright colours. The male stands on an earth mound and either shakes its closed tail or, in full display, fans the tail and lifts it over the back, partially obscuring the head. Meanwhile, the hopeful male shuffles and jumps.

The female Superb Lyrebird lays just a single egg and is remarkably relaxed with it, often spending only half the day incubating. As a result, it takes 50 days to hatch, almost twice as long as other birds of equivalent size.

Key to plate

1: **Superb Lyrebird female**
Menura novaehollandiae
Length: 103cm (male), 76–80cm (female)
The female Superb Lyrebird completely lacks the lyre-shaped, frond-like feathers of the male's tail. Its vocal skills rival those of the more showy male, however. A female's alarm calls and mimicry may be a way of keeping other females away from its territory or defending the nest from predators.

2: **Feet and claws**
Lyrebirds are among the world's largest songbirds and look like chicken-sized pheasants. In similar vein they obtain their invertebrate food, such as worms, centipedes and woodlice, by scratching and digging in the soil and leaf-litter with their strong feet and sharp claws.

3: **Display**
In full display, the male's tail is fanned and raised to reveal the remarkably thin, filamentous feathers and two elaborately curved plumes that bend back and resemble the shape of a lyre, a musical instrument.

4: **Mound**
The male Superb Lyrebird displays on a specially constructed, domed mound. It may have several of these in its territory. It has a single mate, but during the breeding season, which is in winter, it will sing almost all day in the hope of attracting many.

Habitat: Deserts

Deserts are places where very little rain falls, usually less than 250 millimetres per year. As a result, not many plants grow, and there is rarely any tree cover. Deserts are often rocky or sandy, and hot, but some occur in very cold places, too. They are environments with multiple challenges, not least the lack of water. They may also exhibit extremes of temperature, veering from searing daytime heat to ferocious cold at night, and desert-living animals must cope with this.

Despite the difficulties, deserts are home to many animals, including an impressive array of birds. With their typically high body temperature (39–42°C), birds are already at an advantage. Desert-dwelling species also have highly efficient kidneys and, like all birds, they excrete uric acid, which can be removed in semi-solid form with the rest of the faeces, saving water. Many species of birds obtain all the water they need from their prey, especially if they eat the many invertebrates and other animals in deserts. If they do need to look for water, the ability to fly also gives them a huge advantage – a journey of 50 kilometres or more is rarely a problem. Desert birds are often nomadic, moving erratically over months to find the best conditions.

Birds can deal with hot days in various ways. Many retreat into shade, or even burrows. Birds don't sweat, so they remain still and pant to lose heat. Many are most active at dawn and dusk. On cold mornings some birds sunbathe to warm up.

The majority of desert birds feed on the ground and most have dull colours to keep them camouflaged. Many have eye-catching aerial displays, so that members of their species can find them.

Key to plate

1: **Greater Hoopoe-Lark**
Alaemon alaudipes
Length: 19–23cm
One of many brown-hued larks of the African and Asian deserts, this one keeps cool by hiding away in rodent burrows for hours during the heat of the day. In spring it has a haunting, pure whistling song. It may dig in the sand for invertebrate prey.

2: **Desert Wheatear**
Oenanthe deserti
Length: 14–15cm
Found in arid regions from the Sahara Desert to Central Asia, the Desert Wheatear can nest anywhere from rodent holes to the bottom of thick bushes. As with several desert birds, its song has a mournful tone.

3: **Orange Chat**
Epthianura aurifrons
Length: 11–12cm
An enigmatic Australian bird that is highly nomadic, sometimes appearing in a location unexpectedly after many years of absence. They are sociable, usually found in pairs, small groups and sometimes flocks, often in treeless terrain near saltlakes.

4: **Greater Roadrunner**
Geococcyx californianus
Length: 52–54cm
This extraordinary ground-living cuckoo can run at 40km/h and catch spiders, snakes, lizards and scorpions. It sunbathes in the early morning, exposing black skin and feathers on its back by ruffling its plumage.

5a: **Spotted Sandgrouse**
5b: **Spotted Sandgrouse chick**
Pterocles senegallus
Length: 30–35cm
Sandgrouse are renowned for the ingenious way they bring water to the young. Males visit waterholes to soak their specially adapted breast feathers, then fly to the nest where the young drink from the inundated plumage.

6: **Least Seedsnipe**
Thinocorus rumicivorus
Length: 16–19cm
A short-legged shorebird, this species lives in barren habitats in western and southern South America. It eats seeds and other vegetation and is rarely seen drinking. It performs a simple flight song as part of its display.

1
2
3
4
5a
5b
6

Gallery 6

Tropical Birds

Hummingbirds
Parrots
Great Hornbill
Cotingas and Manakins
Birds-of-Paradise
Tanagers
Habitat: Tropical Rainforest

Hummingbirds

There are almost 400 species of hummingbirds, all found in the Americas, where they delight and astonish with their diminutive size and glittering, gemlike colours. Since their diet is 90 per cent nectar – washed down with insects, spiders and other small invertebrates – they flourish wherever flowers grow. Most feed in a unique way, by hovering in front of blooms and inserting their tubular, forked tongue to lick about 13 times a second. Some hummingbirds visit 2,000 flowers a day. Some are highly specialised, their bills having evolved to match the shape of their favourite blooms. This allows them to be dusted with pollen each time, thus helping the plants. Some 'cheat' by making holes in the flowers and drinking while perched. They find what they need with acute colour vision, and their ability to detect ultraviolet radiation enables them to see how nectar-heavy each bloom is.

The physiology of hummingbirds is superlative. When they hover, they beat their wings about 70 times a second, but this can reach 200 beats a second during chases, when they can also clock a speed of 80 kilometres per hour. The wings beat in a figure-of-eight pattern, creating such stability that they can fly backwards and upside down, and of course their wings produce the hum that gives them their name. When flying, their heartbeat rate can be 1,000 per minute, and is 500 at rest, while they can take 500 breaths a minute. Fortunately, they have more haemoglobin in their blood than any other animal, enabling them to take up the oxygen they need.

Hummingbirds occur in most habitats – there's even one confined to mangroves. In particular, different species are found at different altitudes in the Andes. Some become torpid at night or in cold weather to save energy.

The hummingbird family contains most of the world's smallest birds, and they also lay the smallest eggs. In most species, the female makes a simple cup nest and produces a clutch of two eggs.

Key to plate

1: **Peacock Coquette**
Lophornis pavoninus
Length: 9.7cm
Aptly named for the male's remarkable cheek-tufts, whose pattern resembles the eyes of a peacock's train. This glorious hummer is found in the *tepuis*, the spectacular table-top mountains of northern South America.

2: **Bee Hummingbird**
Mellisuga helenae
Length: 5–6cm
The world's smallest bird, the Bee Hummingbird is found only in Cuba. When it flies, its wings make a sound like the buzzing of a bee. It is smaller than a Common Ostrich's eye and builds a nest the size of a small coin.

3: **Ruby-throated Hummingbird**
Archilochus colubris
Length: 7.5–9cm
Astonishingly, many individuals of this species – the only hummingbird in the east of North America – migrate across the Gulf of Mexico in spring and autumn, a trip of more than 800km.

4: **Marvellous Spatuletail**
Loddigesia mirabilis
Length: 15–17cm (male, including tail 11–13cm), 9–10cm (female)
Found in a restricted part of Peru, this hummer has only four tail feathers, with the male having long, almost bare outer feathers that cross over and end in rackets (or spatules). These have a life of their own during the hovering courtship display, mesmerising females.

5: **Green-fronted Lancebill**
Doryfera ludovicae
Length: 11–13cm
This hummingbird is adapted to drinking nectar from long, tubular flowers. It also regularly catches gnats with short sorties from a perch, often beside rivers.

6: **Velvet-purple Coronet**
Boissonneaua jardini
Length: 11–12.7cm
Like a significant number of hummers, this improbably coloured species has a restricted range, found only in the cloudforest of southern Colombia and Ecuador. It often raises its wings above its head before perching.

1
2
4
3
6
5

Parrots

Perhaps more than any other bird family, the parrots speak – or squawk or screech – tropical. Most species do indeed come from humid climates, but they are also strongly represented in the Australian dry country, the original home of icons such as cockatoos and the Budgerigar. They occur all over South America and Asia, but only 20 species out of about 400 are found in Africa.

Parrots are very easy to recognise, with powerful hooked bills, large heads, a bare patch above the bill (the cere) and strong legs, with two toes pointing backwards and two forwards. This enables them to be exceptionally manoeuvrable among the branches of trees, and they often hang upside down and use their bill to grip where necessary. Most species fly strongly, with quick wingbeats. There is an extraordinary range in sizes, from sparrow-like species that drink nectar to the mighty macaws that can crack open Brazil nuts. Although a majority of species are green (and have green pigments in their plumage, in contrast to most birds), parrots can sport many other colours, including yellow, red and even pink.

Almost all parrots are sociable and have sophisticated communication skills and high intelligence. They can imitate human speech and experiments in captivity have shown that they can learn the meaning of words, recognise shapes and even count (to seventeen). They even show empathy. Such skills match those of a human toddler.

In the wild, parrots form close pair bonds and are faithful to their mate, usually for life. They tend to nest in holes in trees or other crevices.

Key to plate

1: **Galah**
Eolophus roseicapilla
Length: 35–36cm
A colourful and popular parrot related to cockatoos, found throughout Australia and common in many urban areas. It is highly sociable and may congregate in flocks of more than 1,000 birds.

2: **Red-and-green Macaw**
Ara chloropterus
Length: 90–95cm
The macaws are classic birds of mature lowland tropical rainforest, over which they fly just above the treetops with magnificent slow wingbeats. Their harsh calls reverberate over long distances. They usually nest in tree-holes.

3: **Ultramarine Lorikeet**
Vini ultramarina
Length: 18cm
Many parrots are rare and confined just to islands or island groups. The Ultramarine Lorikeet is a gorgeously patterned species found only on the very isolated Marquesas Islands, in the Pacific Ocean.

4a: **Papuan Eclectus male**
4b: **Papuan Eclectus female**
Eclectus polychloros
Length: 35cm
The eclectus parrots are so-named for the extraordinarily stark difference between the male and female plumages, which are so divergent that they were once thought to be different species.

5: **Kea**
Nestor notabilis
Length: 48cm
Parrots are highly intelligent, and New Zealand's Kea is famous for its playfulness and inquisitive nature. In car parks and ski resorts it often damages windscreen wipers and will carry away hikers' boots and socks!

6: **Red-headed Lovebird**
Agapornis pullarius
Length: 13–15cm
The African lovebirds are named for their habit of huddling together in bodily contact for long periods of time. The Red-headed Lovebird has an amazing party trick: it brings nest material to the nest site stuffed into its plumage.

1
2
3
4a
4b
5
6

Great Hornbill

You often hear a Great Hornbill before you see it, but not necessarily because of its loud, growling call. This huge forest bird makes a tremendous swishing sound with its wings that can be heard up to a kilometre away. When a pair decides to swap one fruiting tree for another, the whole forest knows it!

The hornbills are a family of medium to large birds found in Africa and Asia. The Great Hornbill occurs from India to Malaysia and Sumatra. It bears the distinctive head casque that immediately identifies the family and gives it its name. The function of the casque, which is an extension of the upper mandible, is not fully known, but rivals sometimes embark on aerial jousts, each hitting the other's bill. The casque is hollow and, in this species, divided into two sections.

Hornbills have a unique breeding system, in which the female is sealed into a large hole in a tall forest tree. Both sexes use mud, bark, excreta and scraps of food to cover the entrance to the cavity, leaving only a slit through which the male delivers food. During this time, the female hornbill is more dependent on its mate than any other bird. In some species it may remain sealed in its secret bunker for four months as it incubates its eggs and tends the young.

Key to plate

1: **Great Hornbill male**
Buceros bicornis
Length: 95–105cm
The Great Hornbill is found in evergreen forests across Southeast Asia. The male's casque is larger than that of the female, and may play a role in amplifying the male's calls or attracting a mate. Both sexes are highly vocal, particularly in their large, noisy nocturnal roosts, which may number up to 200 birds.

2: **Great Hornbill female**
The female Great Hornbill keeps its nest clean by dropping waste outside through the narrow opening. It also takes the opportunity to moult most of its feathers during incubation of its two eggs. Of the two offspring, usually just one survives. Some hornbills chisel their way out of the cavity only when the chicks are ready to fly, but the Great Hornbill may emerge well before its chick fledges.

3: **Fruit**
Great Hornbills have a varied diet but they are especially fond of figs and other fruit. They feed mainly in the canopy, using the tip of the bill to pluck fruit from trees, but will fly down to the forest floor in search of fallen items. Hornbills also eat a wide variety of large insects and small reptiles, mammals and birds.

Cotingas and Manakins

Bright colours, astonishing displays, otherworldly sounds and peculiar breeding behaviour make cotingas and manakins among the most exciting of all songbirds. Confined to the American tropics, they live mostly in dense forests.

This flamboyant group's fame stems entirely from what the males do. On the whole, the females are inconspicuous, and are responsible for all breeding duties, from nest building to feeding young. Their burden of care means that they can be extremely choosy about who they mate with – meaning that hopeful males must pull out all the stops to woo them and prove themselves worthy.

In both cotingas and manakins, males may perform in a group. This is known as a lek, with birds next to each other or within audible contact, each male on its own display perch or in a cleared arena on the ground. The accompanying displays are stunning. Birds may dance, they may somersault, saunter along a perch, jump, flutter their wings, bow, hover and ruffle the colourful parts of their plumage. Some birds, such as cock-of-the-rocks, display in duos; in some manakins, three or more males may take part. Each species has a differently choreographed display. Males may spend all year – and much of every day – on their display grounds.

And, of course, they make sounds too. One cotinga, the White Bellbird, delivers the bird world's loudest call, a double clanging sound that can reach 125 decibels – about the same as a fire alarm. The Capuchinbird (*Perissocephalus tricolor*) makes a sound like a chainsaw, and the Andean Cock-of-the-rock emits a weird braying. Meanwhile, the manakins frequently make a loud wing-snap. This is a familiar sound in tropical forests, caused by beating the wings at great speed.

Key to plate

1: **White Bellbird**
Procnias albus
Length: 27–28cm
Scientists don't know why the male White Bellbird doesn't deafen itself when it delivers its record-breaking mating call. As it sings, the male extends the fleshy grey wattle from its forehead for extra impact.

2: **Andean Cock-of-the-rock**
Rupicola peruvianus
Length: 30–32cm
Males gather in leks on perches well above ground, where they jump, flutter and bow, all the time making weird grating, clucking sounds like malfunctioning robots. Unusually, male duos often cooperate in display, although only one individual gets to copulate with visiting females.

3: **Swallow-tailed Cotinga**
Phibalura flavirostris
Length: 21–23cm
This species is unusual within the cotinga family in that both male and female take part in nesting duties. Almost entirely made from lichen, the nest is built on a branch or tree fork.

4: **Lovely Cotinga**
Cotinga amabilis
Length: 18–19cm
The vivid shining-blue plumage is seen only in the male; the female is primarily brown and speckled. Both sexes feed on fruit in the forest canopy.

5: **Wire-tailed Manakin**
Pipra filicauda
Length: 11.5cm, plus tail 2.5–4cm
The extraordinary display of this forest gem involves the male bending down, lifting its tail over its back and 'tickling' the female's chin with its filaments.

6a: **Blue-backed Manakin female**
6b: **Blue-backed Manakin males**
Chiroxiphia pareola
Length: 12cm
Several males may take part in a display in which each hovers in front of a female in turn, as if in a relay. The female chooses just one male to mate with and takes care of all breeding duties on its own.

1
2
3
4
5
6a
6b

Birds-of-Paradise

The birds-of-paradise are among the most bizarrely and lavishly plumaged birds in the world, and they perform some of the most complex and eye-catching displays. Part of their allure comes from the fact that they almost all occur in the remote forests of New Guinea, a place that is difficult for most people to visit. A few leak over on to nearby islands and a handful into northern Australia, but most of the 40 species are confined to this tropical island.

Birds-of-paradise are medium-sized to large songbirds with strong bills and powerful legs. They can grasp food in their feet and hold it up to the bill. Their typical diet is fruit, especially figs, but they also eat many invertebrates.

The need to be impressive enough to attract a mate (sexual selection) has run riot among the males. This is especially true of their plumage, which, besides being colourful, exhibits a greater variety than in any other bird family. There are many improbable feather shapes – from ribbons and filaments to flags and rackets, which may arise from the tail, the flanks and even the neck. Males often take more than six years to mature into adult plumage and may still have a long wait to be successful in finding a mate.

Being adorned is not enough. Birds-of-paradise must also perform rituals and dances to show off that bling, and call loudly, too. The result is a mixture of gymnastics and outrageous choreography, with birds clinging upside down, jumping, fluttering and wiggling. Some males display alone, but others meet together in a lek.

Females select males carefully and only mate with the best. They then carry out all breeding duties, including nest building. They are unusual for often adding the stems of orchids to their nest structures.

Key to plate

1: **King-of-Saxony Bird-of-Paradise**
Pteridophora alberti
Length: 20–22cm
The amazing plumes of this species arise from the back of the head and can grow to 50cm – much longer than the bird itself. The male makes a weird, rapid sound like static on a radio.

2: **Ribbon-tailed Astrapia**
Astrapia mayeri
Length: 32–35cm, with ribbons up to 53cm (female) or 125cm (male)
Another species with extraordinarily extended feathers, this one occurs in montane forest (usually at elevations of 2,500–3,500m) on just a small part of the island of New Guinea.

3: **Raggiana Bird-of-Paradise**
Paradisaea raggiana
Length: 33–34cm, plus male's tail-wires up to 60cm
The male has among the most opulent plumes of any bird in the world; they grow from the flanks and may be longer than the bird itself. In display, the wings are opened and the plumes spill out as if exploding.

4: **Vogelkop Lophorina**
Lophorina superba
Length: 25–26cm
The male's display has to be seen to be believed. The bird erects its iridescent blue chest feathers and forms a crescent with its neck feathers, opens its mouth and dances from side to side. The shining blue 'eyes' are actually above the real eyes.

5: **King Bird-of-Paradise**
Cicinnurus regius
Length: 16–19cm, plus male's tail-wires of 15cm
This is one of the smallest and most common birds-of-paradise. The males display in groups or more separately. Not surprisingly, they shake their tail-wires, which are tipped with distinctive spiral discs, to impress the females.

1
2
3
4
5

Tanagers

It sometimes feels as though the tanagers arose from a session of throwing random coloured paint over a standard songbird format, with a smattering of iridescence thrown in. They are among the most extravagantly beautiful of all birds, and one of the happiest delights of birdwatching in the American tropics is coming across a mixed flock of these gems and marvelling at each one. They are key members of such flocks, which pass through all levels of forest, from the ground to the highest canopy. Tanagers are often 'nuclear' species, responsible for forming the flock in the first place.

The tanagers are, however, far from extraordinary in other aspects of their lives. Most species eat a combination of small fruits and invertebrates. A good many species, such as the honeycreepers, also drink nectar. They form simple pair bonds, and their nests are unimaginatively cup-shaped and ordinary. As a rule, they don't have loud or remarkable songs.

Their sheer diversity, though, is amazing. They are thought to have evolved fairly recently, and many species have very restricted ranges and are confined to certain altitudes, especially along the Andean mountain chain. The differences in habitat use can be very subtle, with closely related species feeding at different heights above ground, or even on different parts of the same branch. Typically for tropical songbirds, they can be relatively long lived – ten years has been recorded.

Key to plate

1: **Golden Tanager**
Tangara arthus
Length: 13–14cm
The Golden Tanager is a specialist at catching insects on the underside of mossy branches, where it often hangs upside down.

2: **Multicoloured Tanager**
Chlorochrysa nitidissima
Length: 12cm
This rare and declining species is found only in the Colombian Andes at elevations of 1,300–2,200m. It is a bird of mature, tangled, mossy forest, where it joins mixed foraging parties of other birds.

3: **Paradise Tanager**
Tangara chilensis
Length: 13.5–15cm
A common species of Amazonian rainforests, this tanager is aptly named for its brilliant colours. It usually travels around the canopy in parties of 5–20, often joining other colourful tanagers to form a mixed flock.

4a: **Green Honeycreeper female**
4b: **Green Honeycreeper male**
Chlorophanes spiza
Length: 13cm
This widespread tanager is a regular sight at artificial feeders, where it comes for bananas and other fruits. It also eats nectar and invertebrates.

5: **Hooded Mountain Tanager**
Buthraupis montana
Length: 21cm
This gorgeous tanager is found in montane forest at 1,900–3,500m in the Andes, where it feeds mostly on fruit such as berries. It usually forages in parties of its own species.

6: **Red-throated Ant-Tanager**
Driophlox fuscicauda
Length: 19–20cm
This species is unusual among tanagers for being a bird of the shady forest understory. It sometimes follows swarms of raiding army ants, looking to catch insects that flee from the columns.

1
2
3
4a
4b
5
6

Habitat: Tropical Rainforest

Tropical rainforests contain the greatest variety of life in the world. A small patch of forest in equatorial South America, for example, may host as many species as are found in the whole of North America. These forests have stable climates, where it is hot and humid all year round. Many have rainy seasons, when lots of trees flower or fruit and food is superabundant.

Visiting a rainforest can be disappointing – the trees are huge, there are dense leaves at every level and, in the interior, there isn't much light. You often hear plenty but see little, unless you have access to the canopy, where life can explode. Many tropical forest birds fly around in parties, so long periods of low activity give way to bursts of manic excitement. A good tropical flock may contain dozens of species, all keeping company to warn each other of predators. At the same time each species keeps to its own niche – some feed on trunks, some on vines, some from the underside of leaves, some from moss, some from the ground, and so on.

Tropical birds are more colourful than birds in temperate regions (by 30 per cent). They live considerably longer and may form longer-lasting pair bonds, with male and female sometimes singing together in duets – female tropical birds sing far more often than their temperate counterparts. They lay smaller clutches of eggs (two on average, as opposed to 4.5) and the young grow more quickly, possibly because of the greater number of potential predators.

Many tropical forest birds feed on fruit, which is available in large quantities all year, unlike the seasonal limits found in temperate areas. It is thought that a diet of fruit, which is easy to find and very nutritious, has given tropical birds extra 'leisure time', in which their many extraordinary courtship displays have evolved.

Key to plate

1: **Collared Aracari**
Pteroglossus torquatus
Length: 38–43cm
Aracaris are small toucans, and like them often have remarkably large, light and colourful bills. The bills allow the birds to reach and snatch awkwardly placed fruits or animals in the rainforest canopy.

2: **Resplendent Quetzal**
Pharomachrus mocinno
Length: 37cm, plus male's tail up to 50cm
The male Resplendent Quetzal's shimmering plumage and long, trailing tail make it Central America's star bird, even giving its name to the currency of Guatemala. Females prefer the longest-tailed males as their mates.

3: **Rufous-tailed Jacamar**
Galbula ruficauda
Length: 22–24cm
The jacamars are jewel-like, tropical American birds that perch in clearings or near water and sally out to snatch flying insects. They are unusual for being major predators of butterflies.

4: **Black-and-yellow Broadbill**
Eurylaimus ochromalus
Length: 13–15cm
Broadbills hunt by flying from a perch to snatch an insect from a leaf. Primarily found in Asian forests, they tend to build flimsy-looking hanging nests that don't resemble nests at all.

5: **Hooded Pitohui**
Pitohui dichrous
Length: 22–23cm
The very first bird to be discovered with poisonous plumage. Common to New Guinea forests, it probably obtains the toxins by eating beetles.

6a: **Flame Bowerbird female**
6b: **Flame Bowerbird male**
Sericulus ardens
Length: 25cm
Gorgeous plumage, songs and displays are not enough for female bowerbirds – the males must build and decorate 'bowers' as well. In this species, the bower consists of two walls of sticks.

7: **Blue-headed Pitta**
Hydrornis baudii
Length: 16–17cm
These ground-dwellers hop about eating insects and snails. The reasons for their stunning colours are unknown.

1
2
3
4
5
6a
6b
7

Gallery 7

Forest and Garden Birds

Woodpeckers
Great Tit
Crows
Habitat: Temperate Forest

Woodpeckers

The woodpeckers are familiar from almost every corner of the world, with two significant island exceptions – Australia and Madagascar. They are typically birds of forested habitats, where their most celebrated skill lies in their ability to excavate holes in trees, both dead and alive. To do this, they cling tightly to tree trunks in a vertical position, held in place by their strong, sharply clawed toes, two of which face forwards and two back. Their specially stiffened tail acts as a brace to help them hold fast. Their bills are long, chisel shaped and sharp at the tip, so that they can inflict a powerful and highly targeted blow. In order to cope with the shock of heavy strikes, they have a spongy skull that is reinforced at the base of the bill, and the brain is held tightly encased.

The main function of making holes is to reach insect larvae embedded deep in the wood, but the talent is easily transferred into constructing a nesting chamber, and most woodpeckers create their own each year. This leaves a good many vacant chambers in their environment, which are eagerly taken over by a variety of birds, small mammals or even insects.

The talent is also transferred into another skill – 'drumming'. This is the sharp series of rat-a-tats that many woodpeckers make in spring. When drumming, woodpeckers hit but don't penetrate wood. The idea is only to make the sound, which takes the place of a song as a declaration of territory.

Woodpeckers have a long tongue – so long, indeed, that when retracted it wraps around the base of the skull and may reach the eye sockets or nostrils. Many woodpecker tongues have barbs that help grip on to slippery prey. Woodpeckers don't only eat insects, but some also drink sap and use their skills to break open nuts and fruits.

Key to plate

1: **Rufous-bellied Woodpecker**
Dendrocopos hyperythrus
Length: 20–25cm
This woodpecker of the Himalayan foothills is one of several species that drinks sap. It uses its powerful bill to make incisions in trunks through which the sap flows slowly.

2a: **Northern Flicker**
2b: **Northern Flicker chicks**
Colaptes auratus
Length: 30–35cm
A common woodpecker of North America, usually seen on the ground. It excavates a hole in a dead tree for nesting. In the north of its range, where winter snow is routine, it is a migrant and may travel up to 2,000km south.

3: **Acorn Woodpecker**
Melanerpes formicivorus
Length: 19–23cm
This woodpecker is famous for its unusual habit of living in groups, and using tree trunks and sometimes utility poles for 'granaries', where birds may store hundreds of acorns.

4: **Eurasian Green Woodpecker**
Picus viridis
Length: 30–34cm
This woodpecker spends large amounts of time on the ground seeking ants, its main diet throughout the year. It has large salivary glands that coat its 10cm-long tongue with a sticky secretion, helping it to lap up the insects.

5: **Great Slaty Woodpecker**
Mulleripicus pulverulentus
Length: 45–50cm
The Great Slaty of Asia is the world's largest woodpecker. It is only found in wide tracts of relatively undisturbed woodland with, not surprisingly, tall trees with large trunks and branches.

1
2a
2b
3
4
5

Great Tit

The Great Tit is one of Europe's most common birds and is a familiar visitor to gardens and bird feeders. The Great Tit, Blue Tit (*Cyanistes caeruleus*) and the Black-capped Chickadee (*Poecile atricapillus*) are among the most intensively studied birds in the world, aided by the fact that they readily accept nestboxes for breeding.

Members of the tit family are small, restless birds that live in woodlands and forests. They have strong leg muscles, and these help them to grip perches tightly, so they are comfortable and acrobatic in the treetops, often hanging upside down. Their short bill is a multipurpose instrument. Many species, including the Great Tit, make a dramatic shift from a diet of seeds, nuts and fruits in autumn and winter to a primarily insectivorous one in spring and summer. As the diet shifts from meat-eating to vegetarian, the gut lengthens. Great Tits time their breeding season to coincide with an annual glut of caterpillars in temperate woodlands. They have a large clutch of 9–11 eggs which all hatch at the same time; when the chicks are almost ready to fledge, a pair might bring in 1,000 food deliveries a day. They have a wide diet besides this and have even been known to prey on hibernating bats.

The lengthening of day in early spring stimulates the males to sing. Studies have shown that Great Tits in woods with dense foliage sing lower-pitched songs which carry better through leaves, while Great Tits in cities sing higher-pitched songs than normal to be heard above traffic!

Analysis of the plumage of Great Tits has shown that the brightness of the yellow breast varies between individuals, and this might have a link to a bird's ability to find caterpillars, whose body fluids provide the yellow pigment. At the same time, the blue plumage reflects ultraviolet radiation; the extent varies between individuals and may provide clues about a bird's state of health.

Key to plate

1: **Great Tit male**
Parus major
Length: 14cm
The black breast-stripe is wider in males than in females. The width also varies between individual males, with high-quality females selecting the males with the widest stripe. Males with the brightest-yellow breasts also tend to have greater reproductive fitness.

2: **Legs and feet**
Strong legs enable Great Tits to hold on to branches, even upside down. They also use their feet to grip nuts and fruits firmly as they strike them with the bill to open them.

3: **Bill**
The Great Tit's strong, thick bill enables it to deal with a wide variety of food items. It can open seeds, and also crush the exoskeletons of many insects, including beetles. When feeding young, it often breaks the jaw of larger caterpillars so that they don't damage the nestlings' mouths.

4: **Great Tit female**
The female tends to have slightly duller plumage than the male.

Crows

The crow family includes most of the world's largest songbirds, although their voices are typically harsh. Many species caw loudly, although even these – birds such as ravens and American Crows – can utter all sorts of gentle sounds 'under the breath'. Many are expert imitators, and some pairs of crows have their own personal 'language'.

About a third of the species, and most of the best-known crows, are unrelentingly black in colour and have often been associated in human minds with death, partly because they eat carcasses. Many are extremely common around human environments, including cities. The rest of the family includes many vividly coloured and patterned species, featuring greens, blues and brownish pink. These are typically forest birds, some with impressive long tails. All species have powerful bills and legs, and they are all omnivores, but the groups look very different.

One of the key features of crows is their exceptional intelligence. The New Caledonian Crow is one of the few birds that creates and uses tools. It will break off a leaf and use it to impale a grub in a hole and may even bend a stem to make a hook to extract a less accessible meal. Several crow species drop snails and nuts on to hard surfaces to crack them, and others indulge in play behaviour. In captivity, crows have been shown to be able to solve puzzles and they can recognise individual human faces.

A few species store food to help them survive the winter or other times of hardship. The Eurasian Jay (*Garrulus glandarius*) will cache several thousand acorns in autumn, each in a different location in its territory, with some buried in the soil. A single Pinyon Jay can store away 20,000 nuts in a season. This behaviour only works because crows have an excellent memory to relocate food. Their memory also enables them to remember the faces of humans who have 'wronged' them!

Key to plate

1: **Pinyon Jay**
Gymnorhinus cyanocephalus
Length: 26–29cm
This gregarious North American crow is entirely dependent upon an abundance of conifer seeds – especially of the pinyon pine – which it stores away in bark fissures or in the ground. These are its go-to diet, although it does eat berries, grain and animals.

2: **Common Green-Magpie**
Cissa chinensis
Length: 37–39cm
A shy forest-dwelling species, the Common Green-Magpie travels in small parties on the lookout for large insects, frogs, small birds and fruit – a typically varied diet for the crow family.

3: **Blue Jay**
Cyanocitta cristata
Length: 25–30cm
A familiar bird in northeastern North America, the Blue Jay often attacks or harasses hawks and other predatory birds to drive them out of its territory. It can produce a very accurate rendition of hawk calls, possibly to test whether they are in the vicinity.

4: **New Caledonian Crow**
Corvus moneduloides
Length: 40–43cm
This crow, from an island off Australia, is one of the most intelligent of all birds tested. In the wild it often fashions tools out of pandanus leaves, which it uses to extract juicy grubs from holes or crevices.

5: **Magpie**
Pica pica
Length: 46–50cm
A common and highly intelligent crow of Eurasia that has adapted to human-created habitats, often feeding on roadkill. It builds an impressive domed nest of large sticks, usually within a tree.

6: **Thick-billed Raven**
Corvus crassirostris
Length: 60–64cm
The huge bill of this raven from the Horn of Africa is laterally compressed, giving it a distinctive tall, arched shape. The bird uses its bill to dig out the holes of mole-rats, and sometimes to scythe open dunghills in order to reach large insects.

1
2
3
4
5
6

Habitat: Temperate Forest

Temperate forests are found in the zone between tropical forests, which form in hot, humid places, and boreal forests, which grow in colder areas of the northern hemisphere. The latitudinal range is 25–50°, both to the north and south. They take many different forms but tend to differ from tropical forests in having far fewer species of trees, fewer layers and more light filtering through the canopy. They also host many fewer species of birds.

Some temperate forests are deciduous, their trees losing leaves in the autumn and winter. The birds here breed in summer, and many stay just for that season, migrating away in winter. This leads to a surge of bird song in spring, especially at dawn, creating among the loudest bird choruses in the world. Some species, such as tits, take advantage of a huge short-term abundance of caterpillars at this time of year.

Other temperate forests keep leaves all year round. These include needle-leaved conifer woods, which have a smaller variety of birds compared to many woodlands. Other evergreen forests are found in Australia, where the dominant trees are eucalyptus. These often have specific flowering seasons. Some evergreen forests are so wet and festooned with moss and lichen that they are sometimes called 'temperate rainforests'.

Key to plate

1: **Rifleman**
Acanthisitta chloris
Length: 7–9cm
This minute, short-tailed bird lives only in the southern beech forests of New Zealand. A primitive songbird with a poorly developed syrinx (vocal organ), its squeaks may well be similar to the very first sounds made by songbirds some 55 million years ago.

2: **Woodpigeon**
Columba palumbus
Length: 41–45cm
This is an abundant species of broad-leaved woodlands in Europe, western Asia and North Africa. Its fulsome cooing sounds dominate the sleepy midsummer canopy during its main breeding season.

3: **Wood Thrush**
Hylocichla mustelina
Length: 19–21cm
Uttering one of the most gorgeous, unhurried, pure and musical of all bird songs, the Wood Thrush is a great favourite in North America. Recent analysis has shown that its song is actually the combination of two songs from the two parts of the bird's syrinx.

4: **Bullfinch**
Pyrrhula pyrrhula
Length: 14–16cm
A widespread finch of both deciduous and coniferous woodland in Europe and Asia. It often eats fruits and buds. In early spring, both adults develop pouches on each side of the mouth that can hold a cubic centimetre of food to carry to their young.

5: **Willow Warbler**
Phylloscopus trochilus
Length: 11–12.5cm
An abundant inhabitant of northern Eurasian deciduous forests that gleans insects from leaves. Males sing incessantly in spring, and fights over territory are sometimes fatal.

6: **Treecreeper**
Certhia familiaris
Length: 12.5cm
A curious, mouse-like bird that creeps up tree trunks and branches in small hops, searching the bark and fissures for a steady supply of insects and spiders. After reaching a certain height, it flies down and creeps up again.

7: **Yellow-billed Cuckoo**
Coccyzus americanus
Length: 26–30cm
A furtive cuckoo of North America that feeds on grasshoppers, cicadas and hairy caterpillars. Remarkably, while usually building its own nest and raising young, it sometimes lays in the nests of other birds. The young may fledge only 17 days after hatching.

8: **Eastern Spinebill**
Acanthorhynchus tenuirostris
Length: 13–16cm
The temperate forests of Australia are home to many species of honeycreepers, a family of birds that primarily eat nectar. This species has a curved bill, ideal for reaching into tubular flowers.

1
2
3
4
5
6
7
8

Gallery 8

Insect-eating Birds

Nightjars and Swallows
Antbirds and Ovenbirds
Flycatchers
Habitat: Scrub

Nightjars and Swallows

The nightjars and swallows are in no way related, but they share the niche of catching flying insects over open areas. Nightjars do so at dawn, dusk and during the night, while swallows do so during the day. Both groups have large heads, very short bills that can open exceptionally wide, long tails and long, swept-back wings. They all catch insects with their mouths, usually locating them by sight.

There are several groups of nightjar-like birds, and they are found all over the world. They all have brown, intricately patterned, cryptic plumage so that they cannot be seen at roost by day, either on a tree branch or on the ground. Their huge mouth has a soft palate for sensitivity and they have bristles around the mandibles, perhaps to help detect or funnel prey, or perhaps also to protect the eyes from damage. Some species simply catch prey on a short sally from a perch, but others roam more extensively. Most members of this group make loud calls at night, and many of their sounds are distinctly weird, including howls, whistles and machine-like, repetitive calls.

Swallows and martins also occur all over the world and are well known around human habitation – indeed, they will use houses, outbuildings or bridges as sites for their nests, often using mud mixed with feathers for the structure. Many in the family are famed migrants, undertaking long journeys across continents – swallows are the birds that originally inspired research into migration, with their endearing habit of commonly returning exactly to the same place year after year to nest.

Key to plate

1: **Barn Swallow**
Hirundo rustica
Length: 17–19cm
One of the great bird travellers, with populations breeding in the northern hemisphere before migrating to spend the winter in the southern hemisphere. European birds can travel 10,000km each way.

2: **Lesser Striped Swallow**
Cecropis abyssinica
Length: 15–19cm
Swallows often skim low over the ground to catch flying insects. This species averages a height of about 6m and, like many of its relatives, will often fly over water when insects are hatching.

3: **Common Poorwill**
Phalaenoptilus nuttallii
Length: 19–21cm
The Common Poorwill is famous as the only bird in the world that 'hibernates' – at any rate, it remains inactive (torpid) on most winter days and nights and may lower its body temperature to as low as 5°C.

4: **Standard-winged Nightjar**
Caprimulgus longipennis
Length: 21–22cm, plus male's 'standards' of 45–53cm
When breeding, males gather in groups and perform display flights, lifting up their modified primary feathers so that they look like small birds flying above them. This is a tropical African species.

5: **White-winged Potoo**
Nyctibius leucopterus
Length: 24–29cm
Potoos are odd, cryptically feathered nocturnal birds from tropical America which sit on perches in a vertical posture. Every so often they fly off to catch large flying insects such as moths and beetles in their enormous mouth.

6: **White-breasted Woodswallow**
Artamus leucorynchus
Length: 17.5–19.5cm
The woodswallows are mainly found in Australasia. They live in open areas, where they sit on treetops, wires and other elevated perches, sallying out to catch flying insects.

1
2
3
4
5
6

Antbirds and Ovenbirds

If you thought all the birds of the American tropics were brightly coloured, think again. The group of bird families featured here are almost all brown, although many have bold patterns. They are a complex group of songbirds with a wide range of lifestyles.

The antbirds are mostly confined to forests, where they often occupy the lower levels, with few venturing up to the canopy. Many live on or near the ground. They get their name from the behaviour of some species that follow swarms of soldier ants – not to eat the ants themselves but to intercept the invertebrates fleeing from them. Ant swarms are a permanent feature of most tropical forests, and some antbirds (and other birds) spend significant amounts of time feeding in this way.

The ovenbirds are a diverse group that are generally found in more open habitats than antbirds. However, one of their offshoots, the woodcreepers, specialise in creeping along the limbs of forest trees; other species feed in the forest canopy or in dense thickets. One of the unusual features of ovenbirds is that they are found in every conceivable habitat, from high-elevation grassland to marshes, and from seashores to stream sides. They also show an impressive variety of bill shapes, from long and downcurved to short and uptilted, while others are long and sharply pointed. Equally diverse and impressive are their nests, which are often unexpectedly large and intricate, vastly exceeding the size you would expect for a small bird.

Key to plate

1: **Ocellated Antbird**
Phaenostictus mcleannani
Length: 17–20cm
In common with many antbirds, this is an inhabitant of rich, dense tropical forest, where it tends to live in the understory. It is a follower of ant swarms, dominating other species that feed on these insects.

2: **White-plumed Antbird**
Pithys albifrons
Length: 11.5–12.5cm
This distinctive antbird relies entirely on a single feeding method. It finds army ant swarms and catches invertebrates fleeing from them, not feeding on the ants themselves. It lives in lowland forest in tropical America.

3: **Red-billed Scythebill**
Campylorhamphus trochilirostris
Length: 22–28cm
This bird creeps up and along branches festooned with epiphytes and other vegetation, using its remarkably long, downcurved bill to probe into holes, cracks and clumps of moss for spiders and insects.

4: **Black-faced Ant-Thrush**
Formicarius analis
Length: 16cm
One of the many ground-dwelling birds of tropical forests in the Americas, this one makes a distinctive call but is extremely difficult to spot. It often sweeps its bill through leaf-litter to catch insects.

5: **Firewood-gatherer**
Anumbius annumbi
Length: 18–20cm
Not a large bird – starling-sized – but one that is famous for building a massive nest of sticks that looks like a pile of firewood. The nest may be 1m tall and 50cm wide, and the interior is protected by a twisty entrance tunnel.

6: **Rufous Hornero**
Furnarius rufus
Length: 16–23cm
'Hornero' is Spanish for oven, and the word aptly describes the mud-nests of this common bird of southern South America. They are round and about 20cm in diameter, often placed atop a fence post or other obvious location.

1
2
3
4
5
6

Flycatchers

Every corner of the world except for the harshest polar regions plays host to myriad flying insects. Not surprisingly, given that they form a nutritious snack, a great many birds of all kinds feed on them. Among the professionals are the flycatchers. Hundreds of species in several families bear this name. Among them are the New World (tyrant) flycatchers (Tyrannidae) with about 450 species, the Old World flycatchers (Muscicapidae) with around 300 and the monarch flycatchers (Monarchidae) with 100. They don't corner the market, but this shows how many birds have adopted this way of life.

Most of the birds in these families have mouths and bills adapted to the lifestyle. On the whole, for a bird that is launching into the air to catch food with its mouth, it pays to have a broad, laterally flattened bill. Most flycatchers also have bristles at the base of the bill, which might be sensory to help guide the bird as it strikes and might also act as protectors of the eyes and face.

It is amazing how the simple act of catching flying insects can vary among different species. Some birds launch from a high perch, snap their insect in flight and return to the same or another perch. Others launch from a perch but snatch the insect from the ground; others do the same but aim for an insect on a leaf, a technique known as sally-gleaning. Some birds are strictly canopy feeders, others are found in the mid-levels of forests and others at the edge. And, of course, they vary in size, so that some will feed on mosquitoes and gnats, while at the other end of the scale, others catch bees and dragonflies. If you add in the fact that a flycatcher exists in just about every habitat in the world, you can see how this group of birds has flourished.

Key to plate

1: **Black Paradise-Flycatcher**
Terpsiphone atrocaudata
Length: 17–20cm, plus male's tail streamers of 25cm
In this species from Japan and Korea, the male's tail may protrude further than the length of the bird itself. Females have shorter tails, but when choosing a mate they prefer males with the longest tail.

2: **Short-tailed Pygmy-Tyrant**
Myiornis ecaudatus
Length: 6.5cm
Many species of hummingbirds are larger than this, the world's smallest songbird. It lives in the canopy of dense tropical forests and catches insects by flying up and plucking them from the underside of leaves.

3: **Great Kiskadee**
Pitangus sulphuratus
Length: 24cm
One of the most abundant of the American flycatchers, the Great Kiskadee makes a living by watching from an elevated perch and then swooping on any prey seen – be it on the ground, higher up or flying. Its broad diet includes fish, bats and fruit.

4: **Vermilion Flycatcher**
Pyrocephalus rubinus
Length: 13–14cm
Most New World flycatchers are dull in colour or yellow, so the spectacular Vermilion Flycatcher is a standout. It is found all the way from the southern USA to northern Argentina.

5: **European Pied Flycatcher**
Ficedula hypoleuca
Length: 13cm
The male European Pied Flycatcher is unusual for sometimes defending two widely separated territories at once and singing to attract a different female to each one. It catches insects at all levels in forests.

6: **Verditer Flycatcher**
Eumyias thalassinus
Length: 15–17cm
In common with many flycatchers, this beautiful species often deliberately brushes the foliage to dislodge flying insects, which it then captures.

1
2
3
4
5
6

Habitat: Scrub

Scrub, also known as brush or shrubland, is found in the transition between open habitats, such as deserts or grasslands, and those with tree cover, such as woods and forest. There is no real definition of scrub, and there are many types worldwide, but they are often fantastic habitats for birds. Their plants are generally low-growing and, as a result, are often thick, thorny and not very accessible to larger predators. They are extremely rich in invertebrate life. Some scrub communities, such as chaparral in North America and garrigue in Europe, include plants that produce copious berries in autumn, providing additional food for birds. Some scrub habitats are renewed by regular natural fires.

Birds that live in scrub are often very skulking, which means that they don't show themselves well, instead remaining hidden in the foliage. In order to find each other, scrub-dwelling birds sometimes have loud songs. Good examples are the wrens, which occur in scrub habitats all over the Americas (with one species in Eurasia), the bush-shrikes of Africa and the fairywrens of Australasia. One of Asia's largest groups of families, the babblers include many species of birds that prefer to remain hidden in thickets, and many of these are very vocal. Sometimes, birds in scrubland launch into flight songs above the bushes to get the attention of potential mates. Many of the warblers of Europe's Mediterranean region do this.

Key to plate

1: **Scaly-throated Honeyguide**
Indicator variegatus
Length: 18–19cm
Found mainly in woods and thickets in Africa, the honeyguides are extremely odd. Their main food is beeswax, and some species may lead people to bees' nests. They are brood parasites, which means that they lay their eggs in the nests of other birds.

2a: **Many-coloured Bushshrike female**
2b: **Many-coloured Bushshrike male**
Chlorophoneus multicolor
Length: 18–20cm
Bushshrikes live in pairs, and constantly keep in contact in the dense shrubbery by calling to one another and making precisely coordinated duets.

3a: **Common Tailorbird**
3b: **Common Tailorbird chicks**
Orthotomus sutorius
Length: 10–14cm
A common bird of bushes in southern Asia, the tailorbird is famous for 'stitching' leaves together, or two sides of a single leaf, to make a receptacle for the nest, which is a neat cup. It makes holes in the leaves with its bill and pulls fibres through.

4: **Silver-eared Mesia**
Leiothrix argentauris
Length: 15–17cm
This is a member of the babbler complex, a marvellous mixture of colourful birds that live in forests and undergrowth in Asia. This species and many others are sociable, gathering with their own kind and also joining general bird flocks.

5: **Superb Fairywren**
Malurus cyaneus
Length: 15–20cm
The fairywrens of Australasia live in long-term groups consisting of an adult pair and young from previous years' broods. Surprisingly, males and females mate with other members of the opposite sex besides their partner.

6: **Bay Wren**
Cantorchilus nigricapillus
Length: 12–16cm
Many wrens live in dense shrubbery, often on the edges of forest. In some species, including the Bay Wren, males and females sing loud duets. The two birds alternate their part of a song, which sounds as though it comes from just one bird.

1
2a
2b
3a
3b
4
5
6

AVIARIUM

Gallery 9

Seed-eating Birds

Weavers and Sparrows
Habitat: Towns and Cities

Weavers and Sparrows

These seed-eating birds are particularly abundant in Africa, although the sparrows are famous the world over. They have a thick conical bill with a solid roof, or palate, for de-husking seeds. The bird manipulates a seed with its tongue (which is uniquely strengthened by a bony structure in sparrows) so that the sharp sides of the bill can pierce the outer part of the seed, rotate it like a tin opener, and detach the husk. Seeds have a high carbohydrate content (80 per cent in grass seeds) and also release water as they are broken down, allowing these bird families to live in arid environments.

There are birds in the Americas called 'sparrows' which are in a different family from the Old World sparrows featured here. American sparrows tend to build neat nests and have memorable songs, while the Old World sparrows cheep and chirp and build messy, domed nests out of grass. They are extremely sociable and often live in colonies. The House Sparrow and the Tree Sparrow have both adapted to city living, with the House Sparrow found all over the world.

The weavers are unusual because it is easier to spot their nests than the birds themselves. You can see their handiwork, which is unique, throughout sub-Saharan Africa and the warmer parts of Asia. The birds build by weaving grasses into spherical nests, stitching with great care and dexterity, with different shapes for each species. Hundreds of nests may hang in the same tree, as many weavers are colonial.

The colourful male weavers construct the nests and the females only mate with them if they are satisfied with the building ability on show, although males also perform displays to show off their colours. Males may build many different structures in a single season and a weaver bird colony is a lively and busy place.

Key to plate

1: **Long-tailed Widowbird**
Euplectes progne
Length: 15–21cm, plus male's plumes of 30–50cm
In the widowbirds of Africa, males grow long, opulent tail feathers in the breeding season and perform thrilling flight displays to show them off. Females prefer mates with the longest tails.

2a: **Village Weaver female**
2b: **Village Weaver male**
Ploceus cucullatus
Length: 15–17cm
Across Africa, weaver nests are highly conspicuous, and colonies can be seen everywhere, often in isolated trees and near villages. Males weave structures to impress females and in some species may build ten or more in a season.

3: **Village Indigobird**
Vidua chalybeata
Length: 10–11cm
This unusual seed-eater always lays its eggs in the nest of the Red-billed Firefinch (*Lagonosticta senegala*) or the Brown Firefinch (*Lagonosticta nitidula*). The male Village Indigobird even imitates a firefinch's song to attract a mate.

4: **House Sparrow**
Passer domesticus
Length: 14–15cm
This is probably the only bird in the world that would become extinct if humanity was to disappear. It has been eating grain spilled from people's tables, homes and fields for thousands of years.

5: **Arabian Golden Sparrow**
Passer euchlorus
Length: 12–13cm
A step up from most people's view of a dull sparrow, this species is still a long-established consumer of seeds from human cultivation, as well as wild grasses.

6: **Red-cheeked Cordonbleu**
Uraeginthus bengalus
Length: 12–13cm
This pastel-coloured gem is a common bird of the African savannas, where grass seeds are abundant. Males and females often huddle together when perched.

1
2a
2b
3
4
5
6

Habitat: Towns and Cities

Human settlements can be a boon for some birds. Species that nest on ledges and roofs, such as pigeons, easily adapt to city living; others include gulls, swallows, swifts, kestrels and even Peregrine Falcons. Birds that are unfussy about what scraps they eat will tolerate people – House Sparrows, crows, vultures of various kinds, starlings and kites readily live in urban backstreets.

Parks and gardens often concentrate bird populations. Nectar-drinking birds such as hummingbirds and sunbirds readily feed on their wide range of flowers, while lawns, flower beds and trees welcome bulbuls, thrushes, mynas, parakeets, robins, grackles, fairywrens and many others. In suburbia, owls regularly use the many lights to catch rodents. Park lakes are superb places for a range of herons, ducks and many others.

People all over the world put out food for birds in gardens or shared spaces, and in some places this is so important that birds change their behaviour. A number of species in eastern North America, such as the Northern Cardinal (*Cardinalis cardinalis*), have expanded north as garden feeding helps them survive winter, and the central European Blackcap (*Sylvia atricapilla*) now migrates to Britain instead of Spain.

Human settlements can provide other opportunities, too. In arid regions, humans provide water, a boon to desert birds. On the other hand, on cold winter days, some birds such as Starlings (*Sturnus vulgaris*) come to roost in cities, where they are warmer.

Key to plate

1: **Common Myna**
Acridotheres tristis
Length: 23–26cm
This noisy member of the starling family is a familiar urban bird, originating in Asia but now common in many warmer regions. It often gathers in enormous roosts at night.

2: **Crimson Sunbird**
Aethopyga siparaja
Length: 10–15cm
Sunbirds suck up nectar from flowers, so it isn't surprising that many species occur in gardens. This is a stunning species from warm parts of Asia.

3: **Tree Sparrow**
Passer montanus
Length: 14–15cm
Less well known than its relative the House Sparrow, the Tree Sparrow is found in many cities, suburbs and villages in Asia, especially in the tropics.

4a: **House Finch male**
4b: **House Finch female**
Haemorhous mexicanus
Length: 13–15cm
In North America, feeding birds in gardens is very popular. As a result the House Finch, naturally a western bird, is now found across the continent.

5: **Rock Dove/Feral Pigeon**
Columba livia
Length: 29–36cm
Pigeons have been kept by people for centuries, both for food and for sending messages using their remarkable homing ability. This species occurs in cities around the world, and also lives wild on cliffs and mountains.

6: **Great-tailed Grackle**
Quiscalus mexicanus
Length: 38–46cm
Grackles have a clever trick – they insert their bill into the soil and can then open it using their strong muscles to uncover food. This trick has enabled several species to exploit any open space, such as a lawn, park or roadside verge.

7: **Red-whiskered Bulbul**
Pycnonotus jocosus
Length: 17–23cm
Bulbuls are birds of Africa and Asia which, although originally forest species, are often common in gardens. Here, their broad diet of fruit, seeds, flowers and insects helps them thrive.

1
2
3
4a
4b
5
6
7

Library

Index

Curators

Dominic Couzens is an award-winning nature writer, bird expert, adventurer and international field trip leader. Besides books, he writes in several British magazines and newspapers, including *Bird Watching* magazine, the bestselling wild bird title in the UK. He also writes about wildlife travel and conservation. In 2021, Dominic was awarded the Dilys Breese Medal of the British Trust for Ornithology and in 2025 his book *An Insect a Day* was longlisted for the Wainwright Prize for nature writing.

Teagan White is an artist and illustrator living in the Pacific Northwest of the USA. They use depictions of flora and fauna to celebrate the intricate beauty of the natural world and illustrate the fraught relationship between humans and the rest of nature. Teagan is the illustrator of *Oceanarium* in the Welcome to the Museum series.

To Learn More

RSPB
The RSPB's online A–Z bird finder contains everything you need to know about more than 250 birds, from the Aquatic Warbler to the Yellowhammer.
www.rspb.org.uk/birds-and-wildlife/a-z

Birds of the World
A great resource covering every bird species in the world, with multimedia and vast amounts of information.
https://birdsoftheworld.org

Avibase
Avibase is full of detailed information about bird taxonomy and checklists.
https://avibase.bsc-eoc.org

Xeno-Canto
An incredible collection of free-access sound recordings of birds.
https://xeno-canto.org

eBird
The best place to enter all your own bird sightings and see others from around the world.
https://ebird.org

All About Birds
A wonderful place to find accurate information about birds, birding and wider environmental subjects.
www.allaboutbirds.org

Natural History Museum
The Natural History Museum in the UK has a good section on bird fossils.
www.nhm.ac.uk/discover/dino-directory

National Audubon Society
Explore more than 800 North American bird species.
www.audubon.org/bird-guide

BirdLife International
BirdLife International's website is an incredible resource for conservation, covering every species in the world.
www.birdlife.org

Fatbirder
A remarkable resource with a special emphasis on birding around the world, but much more too.
https://fatbirder.com

10,000 Birds
The 10,000 Birds websites is particularly good for blogs and opinions, as well as general information.
www.10000birds.com